A GATHERING OF EAGLES

SECOND EDITION

Colonel Jimmie Dean Coy, MC FS

Evergreen
PRESS

A Gathering of Eagles, Second Edition
Second Printing

Copyright ©1999, 2000 Col. Jim Coy

ISBN: 1-58169-049-5 (Paperback) 1-58169-053-3 (Hardcover)
For Worldwide Distribution
Printed in the U.S.A.

Evergreen Press
An Imprint of Genesis Communications, Inc.
P.O. Box 91011 • Mobile, AL 36691
800-367-8203

DEDICATION

This book is dedicated to all the leaders who have made America great . . . and to those who paid the ultimate sacrifice to keep America free.

ACKNOWLEDGMENTS

I need to thank my family, especially Vicki and Josh, for allowing me the time to work on this project. At times I questioned if the time spent on a book about leadership was really worth the time lost to my family. But I found that the advice offered by these men affected my life in a positive way. I hope their ideas and comments will be an encouragement to all who read this book. Thanks, Vic and Josh. You are the best! You are my life!

I also have to extend my personal thanks to each individual who contributed to the book. I believe the wisdom they have shared was "forged in the furnace of adversity." Without these men who were willing to offer their advice, wisdom, and time, there would be no book.

I also want to thank the many friends who gave me encouragement, insight, and direction. They are too numerous to list but were great sounding boards. Finally, I must thank Larry and Tom for their continued interest, help, input, and most importantly, their friendship.

INTRODUCTION

As a physician, teacher, and consultant in military medicine, I am often asked for advice by young leaders. I tell young men and women, when faced with a decision between right and wrong, to always make the right decision no matter what the cost. And then, with experience and God's direction, the "grey area" decisions to be made will diminish in number, and the making of right decisions will increase even more.

As I look back on my life, I realize that too often I made the wrong choices. As humans, we all fail. With the help of God and a willingness to make the right decisions, we can move from mere success to significance.

It has been a privilege and an honor to compile this work. The questions I asked of each man who contributed to this book were: "What is your creed, your code of conduct for life? How do you move from success to significance?" It became obvious as I began collecting their responses that I was weaving together priceless wisdom from leaders to create a tapestry of advice about success, significance, and leadership.

Some of the threads were red from the shed blood of America's heroes. Some of the threads were white and spiritually pure. Some of the threads were dark and worn and were born from the experience of captivity and torture. When the work was finished, I realized the colors blended into shades of silver and gold. I wish you the very best in your study of this work. May it help you move from success to significance.

JDC

ADDED NOTES

DISCLAIMER

The advice, comments, and viewpoints expressed by the contributors to *A Gathering of Eagles* are solely the opinions of each individual and do not reflect the official policy of any society, organization, the Department of Defense, any branch of service, political party, institution, denomination, or church.

The advice in this book is human advice, but no human is perfect. We may not agree with the philosophy or actions of some leaders, but there is a need to listen to their advice and wisdom in order to better form our own concepts about leadership, success, and significance.

A Gathering of Eagles features the advice of men exclusively. This in no way is intended to denigrate the contributions of the many gifted and selfless women in leadership who have served God and country with excellence and dedication. Rather, we are seeking to make a statement about positive male leadership in a day when the integrity of many male leaders is being called into question.

READER INFORMATION

Contributors are listed in alphabetical order within each category and cross-referenced to other appropriate categories.

TABLE OF CONTENTS

PART I — MEDAL OF HONOR

PART II — MILITARY LEADERS

PART III — EX-POWS

PART IV — POLITICAL LEADERS

PART V — RELIGIOUS AND SOCIAL LEADERS

*Belongs in this category but is cross-referenced in another one.
***See cross-referenced section for contributor's advice and photo.

PART I
MEDAL OF HONOR RECIPIENTS

Established by Act of Congress in 1862, it is the highest and most rarely awarded decoration conferred by the United States. The deed for which the Medal of Honor is awarded must have been one of personal bravery or self-sacrifice so conspicuous as to clearly distinguish the individual for gallantry and intrepidity above his comrades and must have involved risk of life. Incontestable proof of the performance of the service will be exacted on the standard of extraordinary merit. The award of the Medal of Honor has been made to 3,408 recipients. Less than 160 of these men are alive today.

"This is my command: Love one another the way I loved you. This is the very best way to love. Put your life on the line for your friends" (John 15:12-13, *The Message*).

First Sergeant Nicky D. Bacon
U.S. Army (Ret.)
Medal of Honor, Vietnam

"In combat, my faith in God grew as did my respect for the word 'honor.' I wish I could sit down at a campfire with all of our nation's children and they would listen to my words of advice. They are simple words: No one is perfect, everyone fails and often comes a little short of what we expect of ourselves.

"I have traveled the world and have seen many places and different races of people. I trained years for war and fought in the dark jungles of Vietnam. Yet, I know so little, I feel so small. I have searched for strength and found weakness. I have found the true and everlasting strength only through faith in my God. I have found that, through prayer, I am a giant of power and ability. But faith is not something that just happens, you must develop it. With faith you can move a mountain, keep a family together, help a friend, or even win a war.

"If you desire spiritual greatness, you must humble yourself, set aside all your human pride, study the Word of God, and always be in prayer."

Colonel Don Ballard
Medal of Honor, Vietnam
(Received the Medal of Honor as a Navy
Corpsman with the U.S. Marine Corps. He is
currently a Colonel in the Kansas Army
National Guard.)

"Success' worst enemy is complacency.
All one needs is laughter in your style,
A smile on your face,
And love in your heart to be successful.
Always do the right thing.
Amazing what can be achieved by those not seeking credit.
A lot has been said about positive mental attitude—
What should have been said is: negative attitudes
promote negative results.
The most important thing in life is happiness.
Life is a journey. Enjoy it."

Colonel Harvey C. Barnum, Jr.
U.S. Marine Corps (Ret.)
Medal of Honor, Vietnam

"At risk of oversimplification, I believe if leaders (junior offi-cers) are imbued with the following traits: personal integrity, knowledge of their men and women, and demonstrate concern for their welfare; if they have technical and tactical competency resulting from training, and treat all subordinates with firmness, fairness, compassion and dignity—all mixed with common sense, imagination, drive and determination, they will be effective leaders. Remember, good leadership is born of concern and nurtured by practice. I charge you to always be faithful to your God, your country, your family, and your Corps. *Semper Fidelis.*"

Gary B. Beikirch, U.S. Army
Medal of Honor, Vietnam

"I would like to share with you two of the most significant experiences in my life. My experiences in Vietnam taught me many life-changing lessons: How precious life is . . . how frightening death is . . . and how important God is to both life and death. After being med-evaced from Vietnam, wounded three times, and spending almost a year in the hospital, I was left with questions that I could not answer, an anger I could not control, and a guilt that almost destroyed me. What I needed was my second experience.

"Two years after leaving Vietnam, a friend shared with me a simple but powerful message: God loved me . . . . He had forgiven me because His Son, Jesus Christ, died for me, and He wanted His Spirit to become the center of my life. God's allowing me to wear the Medal of Honor was only to open doors so I could share His love (Jer. 9:23-24, Ps. 49:20). Although this is not Scripture, the following quote had an immediate impact on me as soon as I read it. I first saw it in a Mike Force team house in Pleiku. 'To really live you must almost die. To those who fight for it . . . life has a meaning . . . the protected will never know!'"

Master Sergeant Roy P. Benavidez, U.S. Army (Ret.)
Medal of Honor, Vietnam

"Our youth need role models. They need to know and understand the price that has been paid for the freedom we enjoy. I always ask them to get an education, say no to drugs, and stay away from gangs. The youth of America will be our future leaders."

Major General Patrick Brady U.S. Army (Ret.)
Medal of Honor, Vietnam

"I believe you will agree with me that there is one virtue that is key to all others for it secures them. That is courage. No other virtue, not freedom, not justice, not anything, not anyone, is safe without courage. Courage then, both physical and moral, is also the first trait of leadership.

"I believe the key to courage is faith. In combat, I coped with fear through my faith. It's a great source of calm, of comfort, and it gave me great confidence. I think because of my faith I was able to do things that, for me, would have otherwise been impossible."

Captain James M. Burt
U.S. Army (Ret.)
Medal of Honor, WWII

"Be prepared, be positive, be honest! If it has to be done, do it! Don't look back morosely; think back if appropriate . . . intelligently. Seek and accept all cross training possible. If the job is messy— then do it yourself instead of ordering someone else to do it. Trust horizontally, trust vertically, have faith."

Robert E. Bush, U.S. Navy
Medal of Honor, WWII

"My life started with a single parent, my sister, and me in the 1920s. We lived in a hospital my mother ran as Matron R.N. After one boarding school after another, I recognized the want and need for a sound family environment.

"I married Wanda at 18 and we started down the road of life. Fifty-two years later with a proud family of four children we reflect on how we got here. A good life begins with a good job.

"Our basic rule of life is to do unto others as we would have them do unto us. Honesty is the best policy. The most important four-letter word in our house is work. Religion is an important part of our life; however, God helps those who help themselves. With these simple rules we have managed to raise and educate four children. We have nine grandchildren and six great-grandchildren.

"With the help of God and a few Marines, we are happy, contented, and count our blessings every day."

Sergeant Major Jon R. Cavaiani U.S. Army (Ret.)
Medal of Honor, ex-POW Vietnam

"If I were to offer my advice about a creed or code of conduct for life and about success and significance, I would offer the advice given to me by my father. When I asked him how he became a success, he told me, 'Honesty and making the right decision were the major factors that helped me through life.' He also said that before he made a decision to do something, he asked himself three simple questions: 'Will what I do hurt my family? Will it hurt my friends? And lastly, will it hurt myself? If I can answer yes to any of these questions, I don't do it.' He believed your word is your bond. I have lived by these words throughout my life."

William R. Charette
U.S. Navy (Ret.)
Medal of Honor, Korea

"I don't feel like I have much to contribute, but if asked for advice about a creed or code of conduct I would say, 'Do unto others as you would have them do unto you.' I have always tried to live by the Golden Rule.

"My parents died when I was five years old, and I was raised by my aunt and uncle. They were good, God-fearing people. They raised me with this advice, and they demonstrated the Golden Rule by their example."

Lieutenant Colonel Ernest Childers, U.S. Army (Ret.)
Medal of Honor, WWII

"For every element of freedom we have in this great country we must use an equal amount of responsibility. I strive to encourage young people to become good, law-abiding, and patriotic citizens of this beautiful land. When young citizens ask me about my views on war, I explain how war—real war—is nothing as portrayed in the movies. I explain that the ugly side of war requires soldiers and citizens to defend our country, and ultimately, at times, it is necessary to take a life in order to preserve your own life or your fellow soldiers' lives."

Charles H. Coolidge
U.S. Army
Medal of Honor, WWII

"My creed and formula for successful living is simple. It sustained me through World War II: Trust not in thine own self but put your faith in Almighty God, and He will see you through. I had this brought home to me in vivid fashion on Hill 623 in southern France during WWII. Although faced with possible annihilation by an enemy force of greater numbers, my small body of brave soldiers overcame these overwhelming odds.

"Hill 623 in southern France will remain steadfast in my memory. The action that occurred there resulted in my being awarded the Medal of Honor which is our country's highest military decoration. But I must be quick to state that the act that took place on a hill at Calvary far exceeds any victory that man can conceive. It was there that the Lord laid down His life for all who would believe and accept His gift of grace. Through His resurrection, victory over Satan was wrought and the plan of salvation became a living truth.

"For young people, I recommend that they set their priorities straight. Put God first in all things, and the remaining issues will fall in line. Simply conduct oneself in such a manner that if Christ should suddenly appear, personal behavior would prove no embarrassment to Him or to oneself. Be honest in all dealings with other people and share the love of Christ with whomever you find oppressed or despondent. And, finally, to thine own self be true lest you prove false to your fellow men. This is something that has sustained me through the trials of battle and the troublesome encounters of civilian life."

Master Sergeant William J. Crawford, U.S. Army (Ret.)
Medal of Honor, WWII, ex-POW

"Be the best of whatever you are. I read this poem in a USO library reading room in Algeria. As a Private, the poem made me feel worthwhile.

> If you can't be a moon, then just be a star
> But be the best of whatever you are.

"In a flank attack on the German main line of defense on the morning of September 13th, 1944, near Alta Villa, Italy, several men near me were shot. I was untouched for some unknown reason. The Lord was looking after me. I accepted the Lord at Stalag IIB in Hammerstein, Germany in September of 1944. At the time, Stalag IIB had received Bibles, hymnals, and an accordion. We organized a "Born Again" evangelistic-type of worship service. Having prayer services every day, more of the POWs accepted the Lord. A German officer escorted us out of the prison compound to a large meeting hall in Hammerstein. We had to give this up when the Russian army came through Poland. We had to march westward to escape the Russians, but we were liberated by the American army after marching for 52 days and 500 miles on a ration of one or two potatoes per night. I carried my Bible on my back and my New Testament in my left shirt pocket. How I survived, only the Lord knows."

John R. Crews, U.S. Army
Medal of Honor, WWII

"The statements below have hung on an 18" x 24" chalkboard in my bedroom for many years. This is a daily motivating reminder in all areas of my life. Each statement plays a different role in circumstances whether good or bad, large or small, great or uneventful: 'God only is great!' and 'Mind over matter.'

"Just a reminder, consider these things. What shall I do? None of the secrets of success work unless you do."

Francis S. Currey, U.S. Army
Medal of Honor, WWII

"There are two groups of people: those who get things done, and those who take credit for getting things done. Belong to the first group. There is much less competition."

General Raymond G. Davis
U.S. Marine Corps (Ret.)
Medal of Honor, Korea

"Two leadership ideas always come to mind. I have shared them with many, many young officers. As you take care of your Marines, so will they take care of you. Never concentrate on getting good jobs, but instead, go all out and give your very best in the job you have."

Sammy L. Davis, U.S. Army
Medal of Honor, Vietnam

"DUTY. . .HONOR. . .COUNTRY: these words were spoken by General Douglas McArthur so long ago. I took them to heart and have tried to live my life by that code. Though I have been called a hero for the action I took in combat in Vietnam, I know through my own experiences that a man who is willing to die for his country is dedicated, and a man who endeavors to live for his country is committed. I truly pray that those who hear me speak, as I do at various functions around the country, will leave remembering just that.

"If you are willing to LIVE for your country. . .to make that kind of commitment. . .you are the heroes that will help America fulfill its promise.

"A lifelong devotion to DUTY . . . HONOR . . . COUNTRY by men and women throughout our history has nourished the cause of freedom. As we pass the torch from generation to generation, it is imperative that we pass on the understanding of the work it takes to perpetuate the promise. Liberty offers us boundless opportunity. Those opportunities will cease to exist if we forget to continue as vanguards of our freedom. As difficult as the task may be, if we face each new day with a resolve to live for our country, and follow the dictum of DUTY . . . HONOR . . . COUNTRY, America will grow greater and stronger and more bountiful with the passing of each day. I believe we can achieve everything of real importance through these three words."

Colonel Jefferson DeBlanc, U.S. Marine Corps (Ret.)
Medal of Honor, WWII

(Pictured with his wife Louise by his side as he is congratulated by President Truman)

"I always stress TRUTH, a POSITIVE attitude, and NEVER JUDGE your fellow men! I learned early in combat that the Lord saved my life for some reason. Three times I went through experiences which left me wondering *why* I survived; there had to be a reason. When I went through the Okinawa campaign, it was revealed to me in strong terms.

"I was to lead a flight of 90 fighters for a strike on the Japanese island of Ishigaki. Since it was close to the end of the war and Zero fighters were not too active, we were given a new type of 500 lb. bomb with a VT-fuse to carry on this flight. The General said in his briefing NOT to drop the bomb without getting on target. This was to prevent the Japanese from getting this 'new' radio control fuse detonator. I was a little apprehensive about taking this flight since we did not have any pre-planning with this type of weapon. I was assigned a different fighter from the one I usually flew, and 20 minutes into the flight, four of our planes blew up. The cause was faulty wiring to ground the nose pin which kept the fuse detonator from being activated during the flight. The pins pulled out due to wind action since they were not wired inline with the flight path of the aircraft. Needless to say, one of the fighters was the aircraft I *usually* flew."

Colonel Roger H.C. Donlon
U.S. Army (Ret.)
Medal of Honor, Vietnam

"I have found that LISTENING is one of the purest ways of praying. I also have found it helpful to constantly remind myself that what we are is God's gift to us; what we become is our gift to God."

Desmond T. Doss
U.S. Army
Medal of Honor, WWII

(Pictured with his wife Frances)

"I would like to share my godly mother's advice: Live by the Golden Rule and do unto others as you would have them do unto you. Study the Bible daily, for it is God's love letter to us letting us know right from wrong; it is our road map to heaven. He has not asked us to give up anything good, only that which is not good enough for life eternal with Him and our loved ones. Eye hath not seen nor ear heard, neither hath it entered into the heart of man the wonderful things He has gone to prepare for us who love Him and keep His holy law. If we miss heaven, we have missed everything."

Walter D. Ehlers
U.S. Army
Medal of Honor, WWII

"When I enlisted in the United States Army, I had to get my dad's and mother's signatures. My dad had agreed to sign. My mother said, with tears in her eyes, 'I will sign if you promise to be a Christian soldier.' I assured her I would do my best. It wasn't easy being a Christian soldier, but each time I was tempted, I would see the tears in my mother's eyes and I would remember my promise.

"I also would realize I had made a commitment to God. I had no intention of dishonoring my mother and, above all, God. My faith in God, my fellow men, and myself, made the difference. This is why I am a survivor of the war. In order to have faith in yourself, you must arm yourself with complete knowledge of your job. Requirements include honesty, compassion, courage, education, faith, and commitment. I am not a saint, but my faith and determination to do my best worked for me."

Henry E. Erwin
U.S. Army Air Corps
Medal of Honor, WWII

"On April 19th, 1945, the Medal of Honor was flown from Hawaii to Fleet Hospital 103, Guam, to be given to me on my death bed. General LeMay had recommended the award, and it was approved in record time.

"With time, I was moved to within 50 miles of my home. I was hospitalized for two-and-one-half years. I have had 43 plastic surgeries for the burns and severe injuries I received on that fateful day in 1945.

"While in the hospital I was visited by Miss Helen Keller and her friend Polly Thompson. Her wonderful attitude and excitement were two things that I never forgot. She was such an inspiration to me and all of the other wounded veterans. I still remember the letter she wrote to me and the way she signed it in block letters.

"My code for life is: Never give up, and treat others as you would have them treat you."

Colonel Bernard F. Fisher
U.S. Air Force (Ret.)
Medal of Honor, Vietnam

"As a young man, prayer was always an important factor in my life. While in the Air Force, I had many opportunities to call on God for His help. The sheer terror of flying in weather, that at best many times was below minimums, gave me the privilege of calling for help. The day of the rescue, March 10, 1966, probably changed my life forever. I remember watching Jump Meyers' plane, flaming like a torch at the back past his tail after he was hit, and my telling him to dump his bombs and pull his gear up so he could belly it in. As I watched in horror, he skidded down the runway and off to the right. The plane burst into a huge ball of fire. I thought he was probably killed in the crash—then a gust of wind seemed to blow the flames from the right side and Jump came smoking out across the wing. It looked like he was burning as smoke and flames seemed to trail him. He jumped into a ditch at the side of the runway to hide from the enemy troops that were dangerously close.

"I called for a helicopter rescue, but they said it would be about 20 minutes. I went back to the battle with many thoughts racing through my mind. Going in to pick him up was not a good idea. However, I had such a strong feeling, so I decided to take a few minutes and seek counsel with my HEAVENLY FATHER. I said, 'If this is what you want me to do, I need Your help. You have never let me down.' A calm peaceful feeling came over me, and I knew what I must do. My wingmen, John Lucas and Denny Hague, bless their hearts, said they would cover me. They were strafing right along the side of the runway, keeping the Vietnamese heads down. Denny said, 'If one of them had raised his head, we would've gotten him.'

"I will always be grateful for the 'MEN IN BLUE' that I flew with and for those dedicated troops on the ground that kept the planes in tip-top condition and kept us flying. I will be eternally grateful for the help and protection I received that day from my heavenly Father!"

Michael J. Fitzmaurice
U.S. Army
Medal of Honor, Vietnam

"When asked about my creed or code of conduct for life, I had to do some serious thinking. I am a very quiet and private person. I have never felt comfortable expressing myself. But when passing on advice to the youth of America, I would tell them to stand up for what they believe in and be committed to their convictions and dreams. Never sell yourself short, give 100 %, and it will come back to you a hundred fold. Always be honest, not only with the people around you, but mostly with yourself. Be kind to people, and grateful for the freedoms you share in this great nation because of the men and women who have served in the military. Our symbol of freedom in this country is the flag. I was once at a Memorial Day celebration where a tired, old soldier got up and read the words to the song 'Ragged Old Flag' by Johnny Cash. It told of the blood that was shed to keep 'Old Glory' flying. My wish is that whenever anyone sees Old Glory, they take one second and give thanks for this nation and the freedoms we enjoy."

Rear Admiral Eugene B. Fluckey, U.S. Navy (Ret.)
Medal of Honor, WWII

"Serve your country well. Put more into life than you expect to get out of it. Drive yourself and lead others. Make others feel good about themselves and they will out-perform your expectations and you will never lack for friends. Count your blessings."

Lieutenant General Robert F. Foley, U.S. Army
Medal of Honor, Vietnam

"Life has its ups and downs as well as opportunities and adversity. Focusing on a desire to make a contribution to those around you provides not only a sense of gratification but a feeling of commitment and accomplishment. Self-worth comes from possessing the highest standards of integrity, consideration of others and faith in God. Those with strength of character will have the personal courage to carry out their moral obligation to respect, support, and provide for those who have been entrusted to their care."

Brigadier General Joseph Foss
U.S. Marine Corps, U.S. Air
Force Reserve (Ret.)
Medal of Honor, USMC, WWII
Former Governor, South Dakota

"During World War II, God saved me over and over and over again. I have no excuse for being here. I often say that God was saving me for later duty. Bible study and sharing my faith occupy much of my time. I frequently speak to different groups and am often asked the question, 'Of all the honors and awards that you have received, what do you consider the most important, number one?' I am able to look them in the eye and say, 'The day that I invited Jesus Christ into my life as my Lord and Savior is number one.'"

Colonel Wesley L. Fox
U.S. Marine Corps (Ret.)
Medal of Honor, Vietnam

"Leadership is causing others to reach deep down inside themselves and pull up that quality that they never knew they possessed. Leadership is very important in our society today; it is needed in all occupations and lifestyles. Some men and women are born with a natural leadership ability and have taken charge and shown the way all their lives. I believe good leadership can also be learned, practiced, and exercised. Where does one go to learn how to lead others, to receive a degree in something as important as inspiring others to follow? Except for the military services, there are not many institutions offering this field of study.

"Learning leadership includes knowing what others expect and like to see in their leader: someone who cares about them, communicates with them, and sets a good example. Good leaders must also be good followers. Those who want to lead others must learn what is required of an individual in performing that important task. Correctness of self and an unquestionable integrity are the foundation blocks. Other traits include knowledge, dependability, and decisiveness, but overshadowing these and other traits is courage. Without courage in its many forms, the other traits pale and fall short in their own right.

"Good character, principles, and ethical standards are needed and are very important to a leader. Today, personal interest conflicts hound many important leaders within our society either because they did not study the art of leadership or did not consider the consequences of personality flaws while they violated good leadership principles. These are unfortunate circumstances since everyone loses under a leader who operates out of a weakened position. Leaders must remain above the cannon of personality infliction. A man's word is his bond that holds him accountable. There is no gray area within the meaning of integrity—you did, or you did not; you will or you will not. Period!"

Lieutenant Colonel Harold A. Fritz, U.S. Army (Ret.)
Medal of Honor, Vietnam

"My Creed or Code of Conduct was and remains rather simplistic:

1. Lead by example.
2. Don't expect the impossible—but maintain the highest of standards.
3. Always protect and stand up for your subordinates—that is an important part of a leader's responsibility.
4. When the odds against you are at an all time high—daring maneuvers and preciseness of execution will be your ingredients for success.
5. Whatever your religious convictions may be—always maintain faith!"

Brigadier General Robert E. Galer, U.S. Marine Corps (Ret.)
Medal of Honor, WWII

"Just realize that the Lord is always with you. Know that if you have 'good luck' or 'bad luck,' He is well aware and probably responsible for your good luck.

"Set your goals where you want to go in life, usually the top, then go for it. Don't let anything stop you from striving for the goal you have set, and the Lord will be with you. Always remember: keep your word. If you make a commitment, then do it. Honesty is the best policy.

"I claim to be the luckiest Marine alive. Thanks to our Lord— I survived five aircraft crashes (shot down four times). My son says, 'Pop, you're an enemy Ace.' I believe the Lord was with me. *Semper Fi.*"

John D. Hawk
Medal of Honor, WWII

"Whatever you do in life, give it your best effort. If you are honest with yourself and can truthfully say you gave it your best effort—it has to be acceptable. Anyone who cannot accept or understand this is not worth much attention."

Corporal Rodolfo "Rudy" Hernandez, U.S. Army
Medal of Honor, Korea

"I believe in God Almighty. There were times in my life that God meant more to me than anyone else. He forgives us of sin, gives us abundant life and is full of mercy.

"I was pleased to fight for my country not only because I was born in the United States, but because I believe it is the land of promise and hope.

"Finally, I love the flag. I hold it in respect."

Colonel Robert L. Howard
U.S. Army (Ret.)
Medal of Honor, Vietnam

"A soldier knows that he is a part of an essential organization. His mission and his manner of performance help to guarantee the safety and security of our country. The moral basis for a soldier's behavior is his philosophy of life, which is the product of his family upbringing, education, religious training, and life experience, including his life in the Army. Because he believes in morality, he tries at all times to act according to that belief. A soldier cannot be truly loyal to his superiors unless he is loyal to his subordinates and peers. To be an effective link in the chain of command, he must extend his ties of loyalty to all members of the unit."

Robert R. Ingram
U.S. Navy
Medal of Honor, Vietnam

"As the years roll by, I find the term 'success' has changed greatly. I find that I have less material needs and a greater need for time to enjoy my family, friends, church, and prayer.

"I find faith to be both the most difficult to obtain and the most rewarding attribute of life. Like courage, you cannot buy it and you are not born with it; it is by the grace of God. You are able to exercise it and build upon it. You are also able to lose it, but God does not forget you. I feel that man needs to be honest, energetic and hard-working, open-minded, empathetic, and humble. If he has these, he will have God in his life, and he will love his fellow man."

Colonel Joe M. Jackson
U.S. Air Force (Ret.)
Medal of Honor, Vietnam

"When I was a young boy, I became a Christian. One of the things my mother and my minister taught me was to always do the right thing. I've tried to live up to this requirement, not always being successful—but I've always tried. Major decisions become a lot easier when 'the right thing' is used as a benchmark. How do you know what it is? Of all the options available it is, almost always, the most difficult one to select or to do.

"In addition to always doing the right thing, there are many other attributes that I consider essential. Of those I will address only three. One is *integrity.* You must be completely honest in everything you do. Your word must be your bond so that you can always be trusted. Another is *courage.* You must have courage to put all the other required attributes into practice. Courage in everyday life is no different than courage in combat. You must have it to make things happen. And *faith* is essential if one is to survive those moments when it seems that there is nothing but despair. It is your faith in God that gives you the strength to survive when there is no tangible evidence that you can do so."

Colonel Jack H. Jacobs
U.S. Army (Ret.)
Medal of Honor, Vietnam

"I once had a brigade commander who had a great deal of success in the Army. He was selected to create new units, take command of troubled organizations, and do similar challenging tasks. I never got along with him personally; he was something of an anti-intellectual, had little patience, was narrow-minded and, frankly, a bit bull-headed.

"But he told me something which has stuck with me for decades: 'If you don't know where you're going, any road will take you there.'

Never mind that this observation is a quote from Lewis Carroll, the English author; he passed this wisdom to everyone as his own. It is as clear and as useful as advice can be, and while its message is patently obvious to the casual observer, it is astounding how easy it is to overlook. Without an understanding of an objective, without a sense of purpose, efforts are likely to be haphazard, inefficient and, all too often, in vain."

Major Douglas T. Jacobson
U.S. Marine Corps (Ret.)
Medal of Honor, WWII

"The game of life is like the game of golf. Keep your eye on the objective. Keep out of the hazards. Stay in the fairway and always remember: Quitters never win, and winners never quit."

Thomas J. Kinsman
U.S. Army
Medal of Honor, Vietnam

"I try to treat people as I would like them to treat me. I try to pull my own weight in our society. Finally, I try to raise my children to believe in God and treat others with respect. If I can do these things, I will have accomplished what God put me here to do."

Peter C. Lemon, U.S. Army
Medal of Honor, Vietnam

"Each night, when I tuck my children into bed, we read, discuss their day, and then I leave them with this last message: 'Have sweet dreams tonight, dream about everything you love in life, never forget how special you are and how special those people around you are, never forget how much you are loved by me and by God. I believe in you, care for you immensely, and trust you. Always remember TRC. And what does that mean?' They respond, 'Make The Right Choice.' Then they leave me with an example.

"You see, in life, there are only three choices: the wrong, the best, and the right choice. But only one choice is appropriate or correct, and that is TRC.

"Decision making is similar to any other training. The more you train and train correctly, the more proficient you become. If you start in life, or even end up in life (because it's never too late), training to make the right choices, then when an important major decision comes your way, you are prepared to make the right choice without hesitation."

Major General James E. Livingston
U.S. Marine Corps (Ret.)
Medal of Honor, Vietnam

"Significance comes with caring—caring about the people who you are involved with on a daily basis. Through caring, you become significant. Significance comes from achievements—not achievements in the sense of monetary awards but how your actions affect the achievements of others. If those around you, as a result of your personal understanding and efforts, become better persons and contribute beyond their expectations, you have been significant.

"Significance is your personal legacy. What beyond worldly goals will be your lasting legacy? It can be as simple as reminding a child of his/her responsibility or making a personal commitment to changing the total course of society or history. Significance is by deeds and acts, and less of words."

Sergeant First Class Jose M. Lopez, U.S. Army (Ret.)
Medal of Honor, WWII

"I believe the only way to survive in life is with family and faith. In war—during the rough times or easier times—I have always relied on my faith, and it was my faith that pulled me through.

"Time with my family is precious. In addition to spending time with my family, I also pray, attend church and do everything possible to keep my faith alive.

"Without faith, without family—where would we be?"

Allen J. Lynch, U.S. Army
Medal of Honor, Vietnam

"Both my mother and father were Christians who loved the Lord Jesus. Both gave me a deep religious faith. Even when I'm away from God, I know that my sins are forgiven. This knowledge has given me faith in myself. If God can forgive me and has faith in me, then so do I. This faith has sustained me through many times of doubt.

"This quote from Teddy Roosevelt is my creed. 'It is not the critic who counts, not the man who points out how the strong man stumbled, or when the doer of deeds could have done better. The credit belongs to the man who is actually in the arena; whose face is marred by dirt and sweat and blood; who strives valiantly, who errs and comes short again and again; who knows the great enthusiasms, and spends himself in a worthy cause; who, at the best, knows in the end the triumph of his achievements; and who, at the worst, if he fails, at least fails while daring greatly, so that his place shall never be with those cold and timid souls who know neither victory nor defeat.'"

Colonel Walter J. Marm
U.S. Army (Ret.)
Medal of Honor, Vietnam

"God is love. My parents were excellent role models for my three sisters and me. They believed the family that prays together stays together. Prayer, faith, and church were an integral part of our upbringing. My strong religious faith has helped me every day of my life. I firmly believe that God does not put more in your rucksack than you can carry; although, sometimes you think He does. God has a plan for each of us and we are important to Him…born in His image and likeness. Life is precious and we must live each day as if it could be our last. Stay close to Him…always.

"There is no greater love than to lay down your life for a friend. In combat, we were prepared to die for our buddies, our unit, and our country. General Patton once said, 'The more you sweat in training, the less you bleed in war.' Continue to train at every opportunity, even in combat. A well-trained unit is cohesive and is ready to 'take on the world.'"

Robert D. Maxwell, U.S. Army
Medal of Honor, WWII

"Much of our success in life is determined by how we handle our anxieties and fears of the unknown future. Because of fear, we may be hesitant to step out into avenues of opportunity. Our anxieties may cause us to miss much of life's good things.

"We can draw consolation from two teachings of Jesus: 1) Let Him handle anxieties (Matt. 6:25-34); and 2) Fear can be displaced by love (1 John 4:17-18). When we have the love that comes from God, we can overcome the anxieties that accompany very frightening situations. Our own concern for self-preservation, though very important to us, is less than our concern for others we love. This is why people often risk their life to save others (John 15:13)."

First Sergeant David H. McNerney
U.S. Army, (Ret.)
Medal of Honor, Vietnam

"I would offer this advice to young men and women who will be our future leaders. Every person should have some tangible goal that guides or influences him or her with utter disregard for the intangibles.

"God, ideals, beliefs, and a sense of belonging to something good and great, can be an everlasting motivation that enables a person to produce to the maximum of their capabilities a pride in themselves and their fellow citizens.

"For the young people of America, I would also offer this thought. I have read that ultimately the only thing that each of us has in this world is his or her name. What else identifies us? Our name should be one of our most cherished possessions. We are the sole master of that name. What we do or fail to do with that name is our responsibility.

"Finally, I believe that knowledge is extremely important, especially historical knowledge. From this, we know where we were and where we are going. A knowledge of the United States helps us form our opinions of who we are, what has been accomplished, and what we can be."

Hiroshi H. Miyamura
U.S. Army
Medal of Honor, Korea

"As you and I know, our country has become great and has flourished because we are and have been a God-fearing country. I wish that our youth today and the future generations to come will continue to believe in God and try to live with their fellow man. I truly believe that if the youth of today and future generations would learn to judge a person by his or her actions and personality as an individual, then we will be a much happier nation.

"I believe that my learning of the Lord as a child helped me throughout my life, most especially in the military while in Korea. For only God helped me through that night of April 24, 1951. I could not have made it without His guidance."

Colonel Robert J. Modrzejewski
U.S. Marine Corps (Ret.)
Medal of Honor, Vietnam

"I used to tell my young Marine recruits when I was a Battalion Commander that every day will be a test; and every time you fail to do what you know is right, it weakens your character and creates distrust among those who rely on you to hold up your end of the effort. In combat, the battlefield is no place for you to be learning your job.

"For many years, my religious beliefs were somewhat superficial. I became used to thinking about everything except God. Following a serious medical operation, my relationship with God changed completely. Since that time, I have tried to give something back to my church and community. My life now is God, family, and country. It took a crisis for me to get my priorities in order, but with God, all things are possible."

Jack C. Montgomery
U.S. Army
Medal of Honor, WWII

"Some things I've learned—after 80 years: Live one day at a time. Always do your best. Go the extra mile. Learn from mistakes. Don't let failure discourage you. Be forgiving, both of yourself and of others. Always respect authority. Be honest—sincere and well-balanced. Above all else, make it a habit to praise the Lord!"

Colonel Charles P. Murray, Jr.
U.S. Army (Ret.)
Medal of Honor, WWII

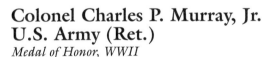

"During my years in the military service and on my travels since then, I have traveled in a number of countries around the world. I have enjoyed visiting their historic places, their great cathedrals, their palaces, their museums, their cities, and their countryside. But I am always glad to be home again because there is nowhere on this earth like America.

"We may not be perfect. However, we must agree that, as Americans, we have been richly blessed. There is no country on earth which is better than ours. There is no country on earth which offers the advantages and opportunities we enjoy.

"It is urgent that the young people of this nation learn to appreciate the freedoms which they enjoy, the freedoms which have been provided to them by others. They should show their love for America, show respect for their flag and other people, and do what they can to correct failures of character and other weaknesses which permeate our society.

"My advice to the youth of America, in preparing to take on the burden of leadership positions in this great nation, is to take maximum advantage of every opportunity that comes your way through education and training to advance yourself. Moreover, you should *search* for ways to do this, not just wait for an opportunity to come knocking. And in all things, always do your best. Beyond this, work hard to stretch your limits. The nation is waiting for you to take charge."

Colonel Reginald Myers
U.S. Marine Corps (Ret.)
Medal of Honor, Korea

"It seems to me that all too frequently today you find that our youth have no direction for their life's beliefs. I'm not sure if this is the fault of the youth or of their parents who fail in their leadership role and example for our youth. Due to our desire for a 'good life,' we all too frequently ignore our responsibilities of bringing up our children, and therefore, let them 'wander' on their own or let their philosophy be developed by others.

"Our youth must be brought up to believe in themselves. They must be taught to dedicate their effort to do right. They must always be faithful to the right philosophy of life. They should not be left to wander by themselves."

Colonel Robert B. Nett
U.S. Army (Ret.)
Medal of Honor, WWII

"I like to refer to the quotes from the great General George S. Patton, 'Sweat saves blood' and 'Wars may be fought with weapons, but they are won by men. It is the spirit of the man who follows and of the man who leads that gains victory.'

"I feel we must use some guidelines from the successful leaders of our past. I want students to know that education is an essential element in becoming good citizens. Abraham Lincoln said, 'A country with no regard for its past will do little worth remembering in the future.' In addition to education, they must also learn to appreciate others and the views of others. The youth of today are the strength of tomorrow."

Captain Beryl Newman
U.S. Army (Ret.)
Medal of Honor, WWII

"Would I do it all over again? Yes, I would defend my country because I love it so much. I did not face the enemy alone for the glory of doing so but to save my men that I loved and were under my command. It was my place to protect them.

"Yes, I would do the same things all over again. I fought for my country so that people would have a free place to live. We can do all things through the strength that God gives us. Jesus was the ultimate possibility thinker. He taught us to see what needs to be done and to do what is right. If everybody lived by the Ten Commandments, there would be no more wars."

Chief Warrant Officer 4
Michael J. Novosel
U.S. Army (Ret.)
Medal of Honor, Vietnam

"As a warrant officer, I am not often asked for guidance. I am an individual from the trenches. I let others make grand plans and strategies. If the planning and strategic thinking fail to bring success, I and others like me will do our best to salvage the situation while the 'higher ups' take their bows for success.

"I have only one rule to guide me in my endeavors and that is 'BE DEPENDABLE.' In that way, I can be a blessing to my commander—he knows any mission he might assign me will be assured of success. He can take that assurance to the bank."

George H. O'Brien
U.S. Marine Corps
Medal of Honor, Korea

"I would urge young people today to be straight forward and honest with their fellow man, treating all as equals; to realize that God has a plan for each of our lives. Place your faith and trust in Him, asking His guidance and you will learn that you can do many things you thought impossible."

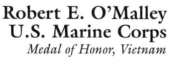

Robert E. O'Malley
U.S. Marine Corps
Medal of Honor, Vietnam

"My father's most frequent advice to my brothers, and my sister and me while we were growing up was: 'Always be honest and honorable.' I've tried to do that. They are good words to live by."

Nicholas Oresko
U.S. Army
Medal of Honor, WWII

"In life we encounter many obstacles; even when life is good, it can still be tough. You should stay with it; it is amazing how much you are able to do at a given moment.

"Your best laid plans are subject to interruption and adjustment, so be flexible and ready to make changes. Also remember, prayers are answered.

To the young, I say—'Stay in school and fully complete your education,' because without it, life will be a struggle."

Colonel Mitchell Paige
U.S. Marine Corps (Ret.)
Medal of Honor, WWII

"My parents and teachers instilled in me a devout love of God, family, and country. When I left home after high school to enlist in the Marines, my God-fearing mother admonished me to 'Just trust in God always.' Six years later, right after the fierce battle on Guadalcanal, I emptied the contents of my combat pack, and because of my burned hands, I gingerly picked up my pocket New Testament which included the Psalms and Proverbs. The page providentially opened to Proverbs 3:5-6: 'Trust in the Lord with all your heart, and lean not on your own understanding. In all your ways acknowledge Him and He will direct your paths.'

"My greatest earthly honor was being awarded the Congressional Medal of Honor. My highest honor—bar none—is, as a sinner, to know Jesus Christ as my Lord and Savior and through Him to know the peace of heart that passes all human understanding. I believe any American with firm moral convictions and courage to defend them at any cost is able to defend himself and maintain his integrity. Valor and patriotism, virtues of the highest order, are part of our beliefs which we must never forget. Since its birth in 1776, our great nation has proudly proclaimed the cherished slogan, 'IN GOD WE TRUST.' Someone once said, 'The evidence of God's presence far outweighs the proof of His absence.'"

Command Sergeant Major
Robert M. Patterson
U.S. Army (Ret.)
Medal of Honor, Vietnam

"If I was to offer my advice for life or a code of conduct for life, I would stress the importance of integrity. I believe that integrity is an extremely important character trait. You are not born with integrity; it has to be learned. Once it's lost, it's almost impossible to regain. As long as you have integrity, everyone you deal with will recognize that you have it, and they will respect you and what you stand for. As leaders, we have two sacred trusts: The first sacred trust is *freedom*; the second sacred trust is our *sons and our daughters*, our future leaders. We are responsible for teaching our future leaders, our sons and daughters, the importance of integrity and we must do it by example."

Everett P. Pope
U.S. Marine Corps
Medal of Honor, WWII

"When speaking to young people, I often suggest to them that real courage is in doing the right thing. We all know what is right. We learn this at home, in church, and at school—but it frequently takes much courage to do what we know is right! I have tried to conduct my life by doing the right thing."

Alfred Rascon
Medal of Honor, Vietnam

"The advice for life that I would offer is very simple: 'Treat others as you would want to be treated.' This is a restatement of the Golden Rule. Treat everyone with courtesy and with respect. Although we come from many different backgrounds, we must work together for the common good of the nation. When we look to people to respect, it shouldn't be because of their position or wealth. We need to be sure to acknowledge with respect those men and women who stay home and take care of their families...the teachers who teach and direct our children...those young soldiers, airmen, sailors, and marines who serve this nation. I am very fortunate and blessed.

I came to this country as an immigrant and I recognize how much I owe this nation."

Chief Warrant Officer
Louis R. Rocco
U.S. Army (Ret.)
Medal of Honor, Vietnam

"The following values are very dear to me: patriotism, courage (moral and physical), honesty, respect, compassion, and integrity. I believe that my word and my honor are the most important aspects of my life. My word is more important than wealth or power. To me, the powerful person is the individual that has many friends and who is a friend to others. My heroes have been the individuals who exhibited moral courage; those who stood up for what they thought was right and were willing to take any consequence for their actions; men who were honest, fair, compassionate and competent. I feel saddened that these values are rarely taught today."

Sergeant First Class
Ronald E. Rosser
U.S. Army (Ret.)
Medal of Honor, Korea

"As the oldest son of 17 children, I have had to accept responsibility for my actions and tried to be a role model for my brothers

and sisters. I believe that one should serve and protect one's family, including the extended family.

"I have tried, throughout my life, to set a good example for
children. If I was to offer advice about a creed or code of conduct
for life, I would offer this: I have encouraged children to always be
truthful, honest, and honorable. Our children will soon be the
leaders of this nation."

Master Sergeant Donald Rudolph
U.S. Army (Ret.)
Medal of Honor, WWII

"If I was to offer my creed or code of conduct for life, I would
give this advice: 'Never ask someone to do something that you are
not willing to do yourself.'"

Colonel Edward R. Schowalter, Jr., U.S. Army (Ret.)
Medal of Honor, Korea

"I will no longer talk of war. My creed has been 'God and
Country.' Although at times I've failed miserably to live up to this
creed, I have tried. The only time I make an exception to my silence
is when I'm asked to speak in honor of those who gave their lives
in war."

Colonel Carl Sitter
U.S. Marine Corps (Ret.)
Medal of Honor, Korea

"A leader must embody qualities which include simplicity, judgement, justice, enthusiasm, perseverance, tact, courage, faith, loyalty, truthfulness, and honor. These may be called the 'building blocks of leadership.' The extent to which they are ingredients in your character and personality determines your value as a leader. There are two types of courage: physical and moral courage. The former is by far the more common of the two. Moral courage sustains men in mental crisis. It is moral courage that gives a man the courage of his convictions."

Richard K. Sorenson
U.S. Marine Corps
Medal of Honor, WWII

"We must dedicate ourselves to the principle that 'freedom under God' is man's destiny. We must not only live our lives according to this principle, but also defend it unto death with the courage of free men. Our country won its freedom in one generation, but in one generation it could also lose it."

Sergeant Major Kenneth E. Stumpf, U.S. Army (Ret.)
Medal of Honor, Vietnam

"Always give your highest honor and respect to your mother.
Sometimes it's best to say nothing at all.
To lose is temporary—to give up is forever.
Always channel your energy into positive things.
You control your destiny—set goals and work to achieve them.
The best thing you can learn from a mistake is not to repeat it.
Always maintain a high level of honesty, dedication, and discipline.
Be all you can be.
Find someone who displays a positive influence on your life.
You know right from wrong; be accountable for all your actions.
You live in a free country. Thank a war veteran."

Major James A. Taylor U.S. Army (Ret.)
Medal of Honor, Vietnam

"There is no substitute for integrity. Your word is your 'Badge of Honor.' Assert yourself, take action, seek success. Education and self-discipline are key elements to succeed in life; however, you will not succeed (in life) without the desire to do so.

"I would also like to offer the following advice to young men and women. It is the advice given to me by my father. The advice has helped me overcome many of life challenges. You will encounter many high and low points throughout your lifetime and hundreds of obstacles. But don't be afraid to make or admit a mistake. Turn a negative into a positive and never say you can't do something. Think about what you have done, right or wrong, improve or correct it, and move on to the next challenge. Through positive thinking, hard work, dedication, and sacrifice, you can succeed."

Colonel Leo K. Thorsness
U.S. Air Force (Ret.)
Medal of Honor, ex-POW, Vietnam

(Pictured with his wife Gaylee)

"While a POW in Hanoi for six years, I put into conscious thinking a 'plan for life.' My formula is very basic. It is this: Life = Goals + Commitments + Plans. My definition of life is: living a full, productive Christian life.

"GOALS: Goals take a lot of cerebration—a lot of deep thinking. I'm talking about two or three major goals in life. For most, that includes the spiritual life. Also most will include family, security, and success. Success, unfortunately, is often measured in dollars instead of integrity.

"COMMITMENTS: These are the hardest as they must come from the heart, and are life changing. A simple example is a goal to be healthy. In essence, that requires exercising more and eating less and better—a struggle every day for most people. Likewise, a commitment to live as Christ wants us to live is a major change for the majority of us. Commitments are hard.

"PLANS: Plans are the easy part. If you keep your commitments, the plans fall into place.

"For much of my time as a POW and in my years since release from Hanoi in 1973, this simple formula has served me well."

Colonel John J. Tomanic
U.S. Army (Ret.)
Medal of Honor, WWII

"I grew up in an economically depressed neighborhood comprised of immigrant families from many different ethnic backgrounds. The value of a strong work ethic was always demonstrated. I learned the importance of self-reliance and the intense desire and will required to succeed. These characteristics, plus determination, insured success.

"If I was to recommend a code of conduct for life, I would address these qualities. There is no doubt in my mind that the characteristics nurtured during my youth of a strong work ethic, self-reliance, and the intense desire and will to succeed, coupled with the determination to accept *any* assigned task, significantly influenced my life.

"These traits were indispensable to my ability to survive and succeed on the battlefields of Europe during World War II."

Colonel Jay R. Vargas
U.S. Marine Corps (Ret.)
Medal of Honor, Vietnam

"I believe no one can be a leader unless he:

1. Believes in God.
2. Always sets the example as a leader and keeps the standards high!
3. Is the type of leader who will never ask anyone to do anything he wouldn't do himself—whether it be in combat or peacetime.
4. Takes care of his troops before himself!
5. Can be patient and not afraid to be humble. If one must brag about himself, then do it in front of the mirror each morning.
6. Puts integrity as his #1 leadership tool when leading his command.
7. Lastly, he must never be afraid to say he made a mistake!"

Gary G. Wetzel
Medal of Honor, Vietnam

"I frequently speak to school children. I like to talk about freedom, the importance of an education, and the meaning of unity. I encourage them to like themselves and remember that, at times, we all have to make sacrifices in life.

"In America, we live in a country where *freedom* is too often taken for granted. We must never forget that a price was paid and sacrifices were made by our forefathers.

"Frequently I ask youngsters, 'If I were to give you a free candy bar, would you eat it?' Then I explain, 'You know that your *education* is a free gift, eat it. Take advantage of the opportunity and make the very best of this gift.'

"I also like to talk to young boys and girls about the importance of *unity*. Our heritage and our freedom is in part due to the unity demonstrated by our forefathers. If we, as Americans, will unite in purpose and effort, in our thoughts and ideas, then we will continue to make America great.

"Kids need to *like themselves*. You have to like yourself if you are going to be liked by others. I encourage kids to find at least four positive things about themselves and to work on them.

"Finally I remind them that, at times, life is difficult and we have to make personal sacrifices. I also tell them of the importance of *service* to our nation. Many of life's lessons are learned when you serve others and your nation. By serving, you bless not only others, but you bless yourself."

Hershel W. Williams
U.S. Marine Corps
Medal of Honor, WWII

"No one does anything alone. Even when we are by ourselves, God is there, often only later realized. Two Marines gave their lives that I might live. To God and to them go the credit for my survival. Those of us who served our country and were fortunate to survive, still had and have our duty to perform, which is to LIVE for our country . . .

"All of us live with these words of our heritage: YOU HAVE NEVER LIVED UNTIL YOU HAVE ALMOST DIED . . . FOR THOSE WHO FIGHT FOR IT, LIFE HAS A FLAVOR THE PROTECTED WILL NEVER KNOW."

PART II
MILITARY LEADERS

RANK

Army, Air Force & Marine Corps			U.S. Navy
****	0-10	General	Admiral
***	0-9	Lieutenant General	Vice Admiral
**	0-8	Major General	Rear Admiral (Upper Half)
*	0-7	Brigadier General	Rear Admiral (Lower Half)
	0-6	Colonel	Captain

"Endure hardship with us like a good soldier of Christ Jesus. No one serving as a soldier gets involved in civilian affairs—he wants to please his commanding officer" (2 Tim. 2:3-4 NIV).

Brigadier General Dick Abel
U.S. Air Force (Ret.)
Executive Director, Military Ministry
A division of Campus Crusade for Christ

"Character counts! Character is made up of each individual's qualities that, in total, form the real person. Here are two that I consider the bookends of one's life and the marks of a fine leader.

"The first quality is *integrity*. A person of integrity is someone who is upright; has sound, moral principles; absolute, complete honesty; and can be totally trusted. Proverbs 10:9 says, 'He who walks with integrity walks securely.' This is as true in one's home as it is in the marketplace. Without integrity, we cannot reflect the character of a leader.

"The second quality is *love*. I have determined that unless a leader truly loves his people, he can't maximize his or her abilities as a leader. God's Word stresses love for our fellowman. Love is the accumulation of all leadership traits. Leading is loving and loving is serving. First Corinthians 13 says, 'But the greatest of these is love' and that 'love never fails.' I desire to appropriate that which never fails; thus I strive, with God's help, to love those whom I lead and those whose lives I touch each day."

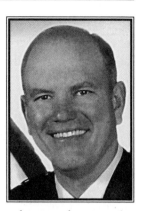

Major General Leroy Barnidge, Jr. U.S. Air Force

"For better or for worse, my life is centered around two writings which I first read many years ago. I often share this with many people, both young and old. These passages are my 'philosophical center,' and have given me courage when I might have otherwise cowered. It has been many years since I first read these stories, but I still find myself frequently reflecting on their inspirational themes. The reason for the reflection is quite simple: As God's children, we have all of the talents necessary to make the world a better place. But, in order to make a difference, we must first gather the courage to actually step into the arena.

The first story you will probably recognize as a parable told by the greatest leader of all, Jesus. In Matthew 25, He tells the story of the talents. To paraphrase the story, a wealthy landowner was going abroad. He decided to give a sum of money to three servants. He gave ten talents to the first, five talents to the second, and one talent to the third, according to their respective abilities. After a period of time abroad, the wealthy landowner returned. The first servant said, 'Look master, I took the ten and made ten more.' The second servant said, 'Look master, I took the five talents you gave me and made five more.' The third servant, said, 'I knew you were a hard man, and I was scared so I hid the one talent in the ground.' The master said to the first and the second servants: 'Well done, good and faithful servants. Because you have been trustworthy over a few things, I am going to put you in charge of many things.' To the third servant, the master said, 'You're a wicked and a lazy servant,' and he had the talent taken from him, saying: 'The man who has something will have more given to him. But as for the man who has nothing, even his nothing will be taken away.'

"The second part of my 'philosophical center' is from another great leader. It was first documented nearly 100 years ago and is attributed to President Theodore Roosevelt. You will recognize this as a paraphrased version of *The Man in the Arena:* 'It is not the critic who counts, not the one who points out how the strong have stumbled, or where the doer of deeds could have done them better. The credit belongs to those who are actually in the arena; those whose faces are marred by dust and sweat and blood; those who strive valiantly; who err and come short again and again; who know the great enthusiasms, the great devotions, and spend themselves in a worthy cause; who, at best, know in the end the triumph of high achievement; and who, at worst, if they fail, at least fail while daring greatly, so that their place shall never be with those cold and timid souls who know neither victory nor defeat.'

"The bottom line is that we are all blessed with our own individual talents—every person wonderfully different, but each with a God-given capability to make a difference in this world of ours. This gives us our potential and our capability. Each able to give; each poised to receive according to our individual contributions. But the richness of life can only be truly appreciated by those who are actually willing to step out into the arena and then make a difference. The Lord of servants understood; so did Teddy Roosevelt; and, to my way of thinking, so should we all."

Lieutenant General Ronald Blanck, U.S. Army (Ret.)
Former Army Surgeon General

"Leadership is the critical element in any values-based organization, particularly one as complex as the military. Leadership involves many elements including knowledge, competency, mentoring, serving as a role model, and much more.

"Perhaps the most difficult aspect of leadership is dealing with mistakes—ours, of course, and those of our subordinates. We have a responsibility to promote development of our future leaders, those who must carry out and make work that which we direct. Unfortunately, too many have a 'zero-defects' mentality which permeates an organization. As an example, there was a junior officer who made a mistake. Appropriate command action was taken, and a letter was filed locally. The officer was counseled, learned from the mistake and would have been better for the experience. But the officer's immediate supervisors, while acknowledging superior job performance, submitted an adverse efficiency report, effectively ending a promising career.

"This is not mentoring, or holding someone accountable. In my view, it's the opposite of leadership! People do make mistakes—some technical, some personal—and there should be consequences. But that is how we progress, and the wise leader recognizes this. We talk about empowerment and mentoring and leaving room to fail, but is that what is practiced? All too often, it is not! Clearly, none of us would promote failure or encourage mistakes. Sometimes, however, that's what it takes to grow. We want our junior officers and enlisted soldiers to grow and, hopefully, be better than us!"

Major General Charles Bond
U.S. Air Force (Ret.)
WWII, Ace, AVG-Flying Tigers

"Crises, several of a life-threatening nature, occurred throughout my career in the military—from a buck private to a major general—but mainly in aerial combat while a member of the AVG Flying Tigers. I was saved by a frantic prayer to God as I found myself in a hopeless situation when three Japanese Zeros set fire to my cockpit and clothing during my landing approach. I was on fire and had given up, but I 'found myself' bailing out at about 500 feet—an instant answer to my prayer!

"I spent four traumatic years as caregiver for my Alzheimer-afflicted wife, which miraculously ended by God taking her to heaven exactly 12 hours after I, an emotional wretch, released her to Him in a heart-breaking prayer.

"And lastly, I gave seven years of dedicated study while attending BIBLE STUDY FELLOWSHIP classes and discovered why I am still alive, and my precious wife is in heaven.

"Thus the following key fundamentals of my code of conduct: My unshakable faith in God to whom I can go for help. The incomparable power of love. Care for my fellow man. Integrity. Never abuse authority. The inestimable value of friends. An established routine of prayer, meditation and Bible reading.

"Some materialistic considerations, of course, help us become successful men, but the characteristics above are what help us to become significant men."

Admiral Frank L. "Skip" Bowman
U.S. Navy

"The Navy teaches you, from the earliest days of your career, that you can do more than you think you can, and that there is inestimable value in being a member of a team. The Navy expects you to seek and achieve excellence in all you do—and gives you many opportunities to reach beyond your rank and paygrade—because, in the end, your hard work is for the team, for the Navy, and for the nation.

"With your imagination as the only limit, imagine all that you can accomplish. Set your goals high, work hard to meet or exceed them, and expect high goals in others.

"Perhaps the best advice ever given can be found in Ecclesiastes 9:10—'Whatsoever thy hand findeth to do, do it with thy might.' You can do more than you think you can."

Major General William Boykin
U.S. Army

"Leaders should remember these points:

1. People follow leaders who they respect. Integrity creates respect.
2. God gave you TWO EARS and ONE MOUTH for a reason. Listen more than you talk.
3. If Moses had listened to the warriors Caleb and Joshua, instead of the faint of heart non-warriors, the Israelites would have been in Jericho 40 years earlier. Find your warriors and listen to them.
4. Take risks—its how America was built.
5. Be three dimensional—physically strong, morally straight, and spiritually fit.
6. It is better to build than to tear down, to give than to receive, and to pray than to curse.
7. When you think you are a charismatic leader, take your clothes off and look in the mirror and you will realize you have dimples and cellulite just like normal people.
8. AND FINALLY, remember that your own strength will fail, but God will never fail. Rely on Him to be your daily guide."

Lieutenant General Paul K. Carlton, Jr.
U.S. Air Force

"'...I have walked in my integrity. I have also trusted in the Lord; I shall not slip.' (Psalm 26:1) Throughout my career and personal life, whether in the best of times or the worst of times, I have believed it is one's character that counts. Many people say that excellent character means many things to many people. I don't see it that way—it is a timeless attribute that distinguishes one from another. You know it when you see it, and when you see it, you want to be associated with those who have it. It is what I use when selecting friends and leaders. Simply put, you won't be successful in any endeavor without developing your character. On a personal note, my Christian beliefs reinforce character as the element necessary to 'walking with Christ.'"

Vice Admiral Arthur K. Cebrowski, U.S. Navy

"Young men and women are rightly encouraged to establish goals and work toward them with diligence, courage, and tenacity. But how is one to establish a goal? Many define their goals in terms such as: achieve command of a combat unit, become president of a major corporation, achieve some considerable net worth, or attain high rank. The trouble with these goals is that on attaining them one is left with two awkward questions: Is that all there is? What's next? Rather, a goal should be lofty, laudable, and one which can be continually strived for but never fully attained in even a long life of dedication. And when someone says, 'Well, that's fine, but what is your ultimate goal?', you will be able to respond, 'Heaven!'"

Major General Kevin Chilton, U.S. Air Force
Astronaut

"I was fortunate to be raised by my heroes—my mother Shirley and my father Jim Chilton. I learned many things from them and from the Catholic faith in which they raised me. One thing I learned was that the best way to please my parents was to try to follow their will. This was by no means restrictive for me as their will was simply that I be honest, treat others as I would want to be treated, do my best, be a giver and not a taker, and call home every now and then. I reasoned that to be pleasing to my Creator I should simply follow His will, which He made so clear through His two great commandments—to love Him, and to love one's neighbor as oneself. Again, not at all restrictive and, in my view, fundamental to the concept of significance. One might ask, of what significance is any achievement if it is not in some way connected to fulfilling the will of the Lord? This measure of achievement is liberating, as it separates any societal measure of success from achieving significance. Hence, being a good father, husband, brother, son, and citizen is every bit as, or even more, significant than being as fortunate as I was to have been selected to fly in space."

Lieutenant General Daniel W. Christman, U.S. Army

"The older I become, the more powerful I find the words in the Cadet Prayer of the United States Military Academy. As advice for life, I'd like to share a few passages from this simple, elegant, and timeless document:

"'Encourage us in our endeavor to live above the common level of life. Make us choose the harder right instead of the easier wrong, and never to be content with a half-truth when the whole truth can be won. Endow us with courage that is born of loyalty to all that is noble and worthy, that scorns to compromise with vice and injustice, and knows no fear when truth and right are in jeopardy.'

"Character, leadership, and values are vitally important to America's future. Lives of significance are spent in the service of others—service to the community and service to the nation. They are spent in internalizing the principles of duty, honor, and country. These core values play an immeasurable part in leader development—more so now than ever, as values are challenged from every corner of society. Values must be inherent in the ethos of all citizens who put public service above self-interests. And the values reflected in West Point's Cadet Prayer will always be an enduring guide that beckons the world and those courageous enough to lead it into the 21st Century."

General Wesley K. Clark
U.S. Army (Ret.)
Former Supreme Allied Commander, Europe

"From time to time, young people who want to know how to succeed in life approach me. I tell them it's a matter of knowing your interests and forming a vision, then doing your homework in all things, great and small. Be proficient. Learn the details. Meet your obligations. Seek larger perspectives. Dare to dream, and have the courage to act. If you stay true to this code, you will achieve success. But to achieve significance you must think beyond yourself, beyond individual advancement, beyond material rewards. Let selflessness and service be your creed. When you put service before self, you will find the courage to take risks, to stand up, and reach out. You will suffer setbacks, but you will also gain strength and greater understanding. When your vision and selflessness inspires others, you will have achieved significance."

Admiral Archie Clemins
U.S. Navy

"One of the most difficult, yet rewarding, jobs I have ever had was as the Engineer Officer on a new construction submarine in

Pascagoula, Mississippi. It was during that difficult and stressful time that I came to my first real resolution—all I could do was my best. It didn't help to worry that I might get fired. I had done all that I could do.

"It was also during this time that I began to formulate some guiding precepts: First: It's the journey that counts. Second: If your standards are higher than the person you work for, then you always end up working for yourself. Third: Know whom you can trust. Fourth: Look in the mirror each day and like who you see. Although these four precepts are the most important to me, in this time of rapid change I have to add another. And that is: Don't ever assume that the way it's always been done is the only right way or the best way."

General John G. Coburn
U.S. Army

"My guiding principle for leadership is people first, mission always. I strongly affirm the worth and dignity of every individual in our diverse society. I believe that everyone working with me is a priceless treasure. My role as a leader is to insure their success and accomplish my mission. The measure of my success is directly tied to the success of others who have worked with and for me. My philosophy is linked to the words of Saint Paul: 'I count not myself to have apprehended: but this one thing I do, forgetting those things which are before, I press toward the mark for the prize of the high calling....' We cannot change the past, but we can improve the future by reaching for a little more than we can grasp. Drive, determination, and hard work can earn a person the reputation of an expert. Therefore, a successful leader takes care of people, fulfills the mission, and constantly reaches for the mark of the high calling."

General Terrence Dake
U.S. Marine Corps (Ret.)
Former Assistant Commandant, USMC

"Keep the Lord in all aspects of your life. Always be honest, especially with yourself. Your most important asset is your integrity. Do not compromise it. It is hard to get back once you have lost it. Mental toughness is equal to physical toughness, and it lasts longer. When all things are equal, it is the person with the determination to keep pressing the issue who will carry the day. During Desert Storm, my wife sent me a plastic card with the saying: 'Tough times never last, but tough people do.' I believe that and never give up when I think I'm right.

"To be significant, one must influence others. That is most effectively done by example. You gain credibility if you personally exhibit the traits you are trying to impress upon others. Express your ideas simply, regardless of how complex they may be. Finally, step out! Do not limit your vision to only that which you know you can do."

Colonel Charles DeBellevue
U.S. Air Force (Ret.)
Ace, Vietnam "Ace of Aces"

"I always go back to lessons learned flying combat missions north of Hanoi, North Vietnam. The things that made a difference to us, and helped us to successfully accomplish the mission and live to fly another day were: training, teamwork, loyalty, tactics, leadership and the ability to follow, integrity, and patriotism. If you are going to make a difference, you have to live by these tenets and believe in the team and the mission."

Major General William J.
Dendinger, U.S. Air Force

"While it is not unique to me, nonetheless, I believe the words of Mother Teresa say what I believe most clearly: 'We are called not to be successful, but to be faithful.'"

General Ralph E. Eberhart
U.S. Air Force

"Three lessons have served me well throughout my career. First, I've learned that good leaders stay positive. Their attitudes foster solution-oriented, can-do organizations. They immerse themselves in their unit's mission, stay engaged with the men and women who execute the mission, and listen to their ideas—including them in the decision process.

"Another lesson is that when we rest on our laurels, we get complacent. However, we can always do better. We can always build on the accomplishments of the leaders who have come before us. Self-critiquing prevents complacency; it puts successes and shortcomings into proper perspective.

"Finally, stay in shape mentally, physically, and spiritually. Do not accept the excuse you don't have time—make the time. You will be a better person and, in turn, a better leader."

Admiral James O. Ellis, Jr.
U.S. Navy

"True leaders blend many traits and talents into their unique character. Two of the elements that I have always admired in great leaders are: first, inspiring confidence and trust in their subordinates; and, secondly, an uncompromising integrity in all things.

"The application of leadership is not an exact science. Every situation is different and demands a tailored and flexible response. The level of personal oversight or involvement, too, should vary with the skills and needs of the team. The truly great leader, though, appreciates that a vital, personal responsibility lies in the training, tasking, and, finally, trusting of one's subordinates as they undertake the shared mission. This is especially important in war fighting, where professional subordinates who have spent a career in preparation will often find the key to operational success in the appropriate insights, experience, and guidance of the commander blended with their real-time, first-hand assessments of the battle. Skilled leaders reserve long-distance, hands-on control for only those critical situations that demand it. We must be wary of the downside of technologies that allow us to command from afar solely because we can.

"I believe that great leaders are also known and respected for their consistency, especially in issues of character. They have no tolerance for situational ethics, either in subordinates or especially in themselves. They are uncompromising in their standards and, while understanding of well-intentioned error, do not demand less of themselves or others in order to accommodate pressure or perception. The inner compass, once truly calibrated, guides both leader and subordinate well. Always, but especially in times of conflict and confusion, do the right thing!"

Lieutenant General Bruce Fister, U.S. Air Force (Ret.)
Executive Director Officer Christian Fellowship

"I remember a retired, four-star General telling me once, that 'I would rather be a Corporal in the Army of God, than a General in the United States Army.' Christ said, 'Those who are last will be first, and those who are first will be last.' I have contemplated this idea a lot. It tends to put into perspective who I really am and for whom I really work. It is important to remember that God put each of us in a particular place, in particular circumstances, to do His bidding. In God's kingdom, none of those positions are more important than any other, but each of us has our particular purpose."

General Ron Fogleman U.S. Air Force (Ret.)
Former Chief, USAF

"I would recommend the core values of: service before self, excellence in all you do, and integrity first. Service before self emphasizes professional duties over personal desires. Excellence in all you do encourages you to develop a sustained passion for continuous improvement. Integrity first, both personal and at the institutional level, is the glue that binds the military together."

Lieutenant General Howard D. Graves
U.S. Army (Ret.)
Chancellor, Texas A&M University
Former Superintendent, United States Military Academy

"As leaders, I believe our role in the world is one of servant leadership, guided by two elements of character which are fundamental for all of us, especially those in public service: integrity and concern for our fellow men and women.

"Leaders must have integrity because we are in positions of trust, and it is important that we have a sincere concern for our fellow men and women because, frankly, we are not here for ourselves, as individuals or as institutions. We are here for a greater cause—to glorify God and serve others."

Major General John S. Grinalds, U.S. Marine Corps (Ret.)
President, Citadel

"I would suggest you tell young officers to lead through service to their troops, as Jesus led through service to us, even unto death."

General Eugene Habiger
U.S. Air Force (Ret.)
Former CINC, USCINCSTRAT

"The number one guiding principle to which all should adhere is integrity. Your adherence must be all-encompassing and uncompromising, as applied to yourself and to others. All other things flow from absolute integrity. You must live and breathe its integral components of honesty, loyalty, responsibility for your actions, compassion, genuine respect for others, and a strict moral code. Those who follow this exacting ethical standard while traversing the minefields of life are rightly accorded unqualified respect."

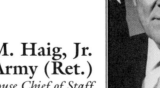

General Alexander M. Haig, Jr.
U.S. Army (Ret.)
Former White House Chief of Staff

"In an era when so many appear to put self above God and country, I often reflect on my personal definition of patriotism. To me patriotism has always been an expression of the willingness of an individual to dedicate a certain portion of himself, his talents, and energies to something beyond himself. To adopt for himself the basic values that have made our nation what it is, and to be willing to struggle—and if necessary, to fight—for these values."

General William Hartzog
U.S. Army (Ret.)
Former Commander, TRADOC

"Significance is something that is ascribed by the future. Something, or someone, becomes significant when judged against his or her environment or against a set of challenges. In that respect, it is awfully difficult to work to become significant. You can however, work to become successful.

"You can make a difference. It takes competence, confidence, and courage. *Competence*: life requires study, thought, consideration. I urge you to read, watch, think, and then apply yourself to your life, your family, your profession, your fellows. *Confidence*: when asked to contribute, in whatever capacity, do so. And do so with the knowledge that you have properly prepared yourself. *Courage:* do what's right. Every day. No exceptions. Be true to yourself. Be true to your fellows. Be true to your faith."

Brigadier General John Harvey
U.S. Air Force Reserve (Ret.)

"Everything worthwhile must be built on a secure foundation. Directional control, balance, and some source of personal power are the keys to success, once you have your foundation solidly beneath you.

"For me, the keys to all these things began with my faith in God. He gave us all a creation full of wonder and beauty, but also of danger and pain. He gave me talents and weaknesses. His love and guidance for me were the core and directional control of my life. However, bad goals and bad actions tried to lead me off track. When I asked, God's love and guidance always brought me back. Without a strong foundation, you may be lost.

"America was created out of principle and has provided ideals of civilized life to the world for over 200 years. This was my temporal foundation and became my passion. Without passion to ignite your power, significant achievements are not possible. Everyone must find a passion if they wish to find success.

"Seeking balance in life is the most practical advice I can give anyone. The Bible is full of life-balancing guidance, but there are other sources like parents, the Boy Scouts or Girl Scouts, and the great leaders of history. The celebrities of society are rarely good sources. Power is needed to carry you through pain, misdirection, and out of balance conditions. While power originates outside of us, it must find a home within us. If you look within, and power cannot be found, you may have a bad foundation."

General Richard E. Hawley
U.S. Air Force (Ret.)
Former Commander ACC

"I have been guided throughout my adult life by lessons that I learned from my parents, from inspired military leaders with whom I have served, from some not so inspired 'leaders' that I've known, and from keen awareness of my own failings and weaknesses. Work hard, be honest in all that you do, and respect others for who they are—God's children. Have humility to understand that you can be wrong; keep an open mind to others' ideas—they can be right. Protect your reputation with ferocity—it is the only currency you own. Integrity and reputation are two sides of the same coin. Selfless service is its own reward. If a thing is worth doing at all it is worth doing right. Anything about which you care deeply is also a thing worth fighting for passionately."

Brigadier General Mack Hill
U.S. Army (Ret.)
Former Commander Madigan Army Med. Ctr.

"It is not by chance that throughout my life I have been guided by early lessons learned from my parents. The value of these lessons and their impact on my life have become more apparent in time as I've matured. What was passed on was a life philosophy so basic and simple, that if practiced, guarantees success. The following has served me well for 32 years in our armed forces: Let God's teachings be the source of your strength; treat others as you would have them treat you; be positive in all you do—look for ways to say yes, rather than looking for ways to say no; do what is right every day, legally, and morally; when things are going well stick around—they will get worse; likewise, when things are going bad—stick around, they will get better; respect the rights and dignity of others; be accountable for your actions; do not live in the past; put in a day's work for a day's pay; and learn to say you are sorry."

Rear Admiral A. Byron Holderby Jr., U.S. Navy

"It would be difficult, I think, to have a code of conduct that doesn't begin with God. Values, leadership principles, strategy—all have the goal of being better or more successful or victorious. These have not only been goals of honorable men and women, but have been sought after by some of history's greatest villains.

"For a value to be eternal, a leadership principle to be inspiring, or a victory to become permanent, they must emanate not from an individual's ambition, but from God's love for His creation. To settle for less is to settle for that which is shallow or transitory. It is a desire to serve courageously and honorably, and to be committed to this purpose of God's rather than our own purpose that is the point of divergence between a code of conduct that has significance and one that is merely successful."

Colonel Travis Hoover U.S. Air Force (Ret.)

Pilot crew #2, Doolittle Tokyo Raid

"Both as a child and during my growing-up years, my mother taught me about bravery and courage. She frequently admonished me to always have the courage to do the right thing regardless of the cost. Then, she would hasten to add, 'You will know the right thing to do.'

"There have been many things that have had a profound affect on my life and actions, but none compare with patriotism and the commitment to have the courage to do the right thing.

"Courage begins with what many have already said or written: Put God first, then country, and both above self. May it always be so with our faith, our country, and in our lives. May God bless all three."

Major General Evan "Curly" Hultman, AUS (Ret.)

"Dream dreams and set goals but realize that seemingly small steps make all the difference. At the moment of success when the dream has come true and the goal met, one understands and appreciates that it was the assistance of many that made it possible. The greatest satisfaction is sharing another's success, knowing your contribution along the way may have made the difference."

Admiral Jay Johnson
U.S. Navy (Ret.)
Former Chief Naval Operations

"My creed or code of conduct can be expressed in the core values of the Navy: honor, courage, and commitment. We must conduct ourselves in the highest ethical manner in all relationships and we have to abide by an uncompromising code of integrity. We must have the courage to meet the demands of our profession and the mission when it is hazardous, demanding, and otherwise difficult. Courage is also the value that gives us the moral and mental strength to do what is right, even in the face of personal or professional adversity.

"We must respect all people without regard to race, religion, or gender and treat every individual with human dignity. We must be committed to positive change and constant improvements; exhibit the highest degree of moral character, technical excellence, quality, and competence in what we have been trained to do.

"Finally, to address leadership, we must keep in mind that reality says there are no perfect people. If our definition of a good leader is someone who has never made a mistake, we're way off the mark. We're never going to find that person. The key is being able to learn from our mistakes and press on."

General James L. Jones
U.S. Marine Corps

"Being a leader requires dedication, a willingness to accept responsibility, and an eagerness to seek self-improvement. It calls for setting an example that leaves no doubt that your character and integrity are above reproach.

"It is easy to set this example if you possess the strength of your convictions. These convictions should guide your everyday actions. Good principles, such as a steadfast resolve to be truthful in all circumstances, should inspire a strong belief in the inherent worth of the principle itself. Ideals that imbue men and women with this degree of resolution should never be compromised when a situation becomes difficult or trying.

"Finally, it is crucial that leaders recognize and accept that leadership is about *people*. They are all different, with unique situations and goals that potentially affect the outcome of your tasks or mission. Leaders must always be aware that their decisions affect the lives of those they lead. Balancing individual concerns and needs against the requirements of the organization is where a leader truly applies all of his or her leadership skills."

General William F. Kernan
U.S. Army

"Life and leadership are based on values and choices. An effective leader is one who is the embodiment of the standards desired in the organization. Positive leadership starts with how people are treated, empowering them with the requisite authority to discharge their responsibilities, and underwriting (and correcting) honest mistakes. A leader must have moral, physical, and spiritual courage to do what is right—not what is popular—but what is right."

General Walter Kross
U.S. Air Force (Ret.)
Former CINC USCINCTRANS

"A leader should be credible with the men and women he leads. He should know his mission, and excite and inspire others with his passion for it. He should be approachable, listen to new ideas, and make sure that everyone knows that they have a stake in the team or unit's success. A leader should be tireless, humble, and of the highest integrity—without integrity a leader is nothing. The leader must be competent at his craft and set high standards for the function of the unit. But above all else, the leader must instill trust—his men and women must trust him (or her) to lead, and lead well."

General Charles C. Krulak
U.S. Marine Corps (Ret.)
Former Commandant USMC

"Honor, courage, and commitment are the core values of our beloved Marine Corps. From them we derive our strength, and in them we unite in purpose and resolution. They are the character of our Corps, a legacy of selfless service passed to us by the Marines of yesteryear, lived by the Marines of today, and proffered to the Marines of tomorrow. They burn within the heart of every man or woman who has ever worn the Eagle, Globe and Anchor…and they are woven throughout the fabric of our institution.

"Marines epitomize that which is good about our nation and personify the ideals upon which it was founded. Honor, courage, and commitment are not just words; they frame the way we live and act as Marines. There is no room in the Marine Corps for situational ethics or situational morality."

Lieutenant General Victor H.
Krulak, U.S. Marine Corps
(Ret.)

"Treat others as you wish to be treated yourself. Believe in your subordinates. Trust them and they will rarely disappoint you."

Admiral C.R. Larson
U.S. Navy (Ret.)
Former Superintendent, U.S. Naval Academy

"I continue to remind our midshipmen that to be effective leaders, they must strive to become technically proficient and to know their jobs. It is only by knowing their jobs that they will have the credibility necessary to lead others. I also tell them to know their people. A leader must get to know the people who work for them, so that those subordinates will become much more effective and productive.

"And finally, I tell our midshipmen that the most important thing which they can possess as part of their character is integrity. This is the one thing which can never be taken away from them and the one thing which they must protect at all costs.

"During my tour as Superintendent, I set out to create principles by which midshipmen should strive to live their daily lives—not just as midshipmen and officers but as individuals who are part of our society's structure. These are the guidelines that I would recommend:

1. Uphold the standards of the Naval Academy.
2. Be a person of integrity.
3. Lead by example (meet the standard to which you are holding others).
4. Strive for excellence without arrogance.
5. Do your best.
6. Treat everyone with dignity and respect.
7. Tolerate honest mistakes from people who are doing their best.
8. Seek the truth.
9. Speak well of others.
10. Keep a sense of humor and be able to laugh at yourself."

Vice Admiral Conrad Lautenbacher, U.S. Navy

"I would like to share some words written by my high school principal many years ago: 'As we live through the hectic tenseness of today, we read of acts of heroism by people who exhibit a spirit of sacrifice and unselfish devotion to duty or a noble cause.' I surely have. In spite of the prophets of doom, there is a strong feeling that a world of peace is possible in which the brotherhood of man can be ours if we sincerely want it and are willing to work and live for it."

Admiral James M. Loy U.S. Coast Guard

"The leadership of the Coast Guard is based upon an absolute commitment to our core values of honor, respect, and devotion to duty. These values possess four essential characteristics. The first is the unshakable conviction that we are organized to undertake a noble work. The second characteristic is an honest humility that encourages us to attach ourselves to larger purposes. The third element of this leadership spirit is adaptation—the willingness to disrupt the status quo even when things are going well. The fourth and final element is the spirit of optimism.

"The leadership of the Coast Guard is alive and well when we believe our work is noble...when our humility allows us to join together in larger enterprises...when we adapt to the next set of challenges...when we believe our efforts will make a difference for America...and when we act accordingly."

Colonel Charles E. McGee
U.S. Air Force (Ret.)
National President, Tuskegee Airman
WWII, Korea, RVN

"As a youngster, I learned from the adage, 'Turn the other cheek before striking back.' Respect is something earned—not demanded. It applies to physical and verbal action. In my youth, I learned the oath to 'do my best to do my duty to God and my country.' The order is exactly right: put God first, then country, and both above self. High character and moral value are what the services are asking of leaders, and they are matters outside the realm of education and technical qualification earned in achieving diplomas. Selflessness must be a lifetime effort!"

Lieutenant General Dan K. McNeill, U.S. Army

"Simplicity has always served me well. Consequently, my advice would be: know what your job is and work hard at that job. These concepts have worked well. Of all the dynamics of the military profession, I find none to be more significant that the human dimension. Every soldier has a mother, a father, and a family. As leaders, we have been given the sacred trust of directing our future leaders."

General Montgomery Meigs U.S. Army

"When uncertainty reigns and doubt is in the wind, these simple rules seem to work the best:
- If it's dumb, it's not our policy.
- You get what you settle for, so never walk away from a deficiency.
- WE not I...who dares wins.
- For leaders, the glass must always be half full.
- Go with your gut and do what's right: you will sleep better at night and you'll respect the person you shave in the morning.
- If you don't take time to smell the roses, your people won't and you will get stale.

"As you do your business, remember that the rules haven't changed much since the following words were written in the 5th century B.C. in Ping Fa, the Chinese military code:

"The general must be first in the toils and fatigue of the army. In the heat of summer, he does not spread his parasol nor in the cold of winter don thick clothing. In dangerous places he must dismount and walk. He waits until the army's wells have been dug and only then drinks; until the army's food is cooked, before he eats; until the army's fortifications have been completed, to shelter himself."

General Richard B. Myers
U.S. Air Force

"Never forget, it's an honor and a privilege to lead, especially in defense of this great nation. To continually earn this opportunity, a good leader must remain above reproach, a role model to those around him. We rarely tread new ground; expect at least a few footsteps ahead of yours. While you should be yourself, be willing to learn—both the good and the bad—from those who came before.

"When you're entrusted to lead others, just do it! Seek their counsel, take responsibility for their actions, and nurture our future leaders. Be out front making good things happen. Dispense rewards and punishments; your people expect you to do both. Ultimately, you must have the confidence and the passion to make a difference.

'Remember, no matter who you are, you stand on the shoulders of giants. Your predecessors and mentors helped mold you; your subordinates sustain you. So you may as well not spend too much time reading your own press."

General Lloyd Newton
U.S. Air Force (Ret.)
Former Commander, Air Education And Training Command

"As I reflect on my life, I recognize three guiding principles that have shaped and directed my personal development. First, my parents taught me early on that it was important to treat others, no matter who they are, with dignity and respect. They taught me that the Golden Rule is a principle by which we should all live. I have tried to follow this teaching and found that it has served me exceptionally well. To be successful, each member must feel that they are a valuable part of the team. This is especially important in the military.

"Second, always strive to learn something new. If we are not learning something new each day, we should consider it an incomplete day. We are always afraid of the unknown. Therefore, the more we learn, the more at peace we are with ourselves, and the more harmonious we are with our environment. Education is one of the fundamental tenets of our nation. Consequently, learning both formally and informally should be one of the fundamental tenets of our lives.

"Third, render service to your nation and fellow man. I am convinced that our lives are more fulfilled and we are more successful when we give back to the nation and the people. I chose to serve because it helps to keep a great nation strong. This nation has provided me with so much for so long, the least I can do is to give a little back. Serving the nation and mankind are noble endeavors."

General Colin Powell
U.S. Army (Ret.)
Former Chairman, Joint Chiefs of Staff
United States Secretary of State

"I'll never forget when I was confirmed, the bishop laid his hands on my head and intoned, 'Defend, O Lord, this child with Thy heavenly grace; that he may continue Thine forever; and daily increase in Thy Holy Spirit more and more, until he comes unto Thy everlasting Kingdom. Amen.' These words gave me a deep assurance and every year thereafter when I heard this supplication, that feeling of God's watching over me was reaffirmed. Along with it was a sense of needing to live up to His expectation.

"A key to leadership is the belief in and support of our Constitution and its Bill of Rights: '...all men are created equal...they are endowed by their Creator with certain inalienable Rights, that among these rights are life, liberty, and the pursuit of Happiness.' I believe in the country we live in; I believe in the fundamental goodness of people; I believe in my family; I believe in myself; I believe that God gave us life to use for a purpose."

Admiral J. Paul Reason
U.S. Navy (Ret.)
Former CINC, U.S. Atlantic Fleet

"The formula for success in life is not contained in the genes; it's found in YOU. There is always someone in our lives who will tell us to succeed. The question is, do we choose to follow the order? We must respond with positive action in order to succeed.

"You are who you are. You do what you do. You accomplish what you choose to accomplish through faith in yourself, knowing you can succeed, then doing the very best job you are capable of doing. You must do that yourself.

"We all have challenges to face. It is our response to those challenges that distinguish us from others."

Vice Admiral J. Scott Redd
U.S. Navy (Ret.)
Former Director, Strategic Plans & Policy (J-5)

"My current 'life verse' is taken from the Old Testament book of Proverbs, Chapter 3, verses 5 and 6: 'Trust in the Lord with all your heart and lean not on your own understanding. In all your ways acknowledge Him and He will establish your path.' Professionally, the core skill of a military officer is leadership. While we do many things, fundamentally we are in the leadership business. Two decades ago, I began searching the Scriptures for God's perspective on leadership. That effort continues today and is summarized in an acronym, VECTOR, which endeavors to capture fundamental biblical principles of leadership. In a very abbreviated form, VECTOR, with representative references, refers to:

- *Vision.* 'Where there is no vision, the people perish.' (Proverbs 29:19)
- *Excellence.* 'And whatever you do, do it heartily, as to the Lord, not to men.' (Colossians 3:23)
- *Character.* 'When the righteous are in authority, the people rejoice.' (Proverbs 29:2; also I Timothy 3:1-12 and Titus 1:5-9)
- *Teamwork.* 'Any kingdom divided against itself is laid waste, and a house divided against itself will not stand.' (Luke 11:17)
- *Organization.* The chain of command remains the best organizational model. (Exodus 18)
- *Respect.* 'Let every soul be subject to the governing authorities. For there is no authority except from God, and the authorities which exist are appointed by God.' (Romans 13:1)

General Dennis Reimer
U.S. Army (Ret.)
Former Army Chief of Staff

"Duty, selfless service, courage, respect, loyalty, integrity, and honor are core values of the U.S. Army. Integrity encompasses the sum total of a person's set of values, his private moral code. A breach of any of these values will damage the integrity of the individual."

Lieutenant General John M. Riggs, U.S. Army

"As I pause to reflect on my 35 years in the U.S. Army, my fundamental philosophical foundation was most significantly shaped by my early years of schooling and service as a junior noncommissioned officer. It was at that point I formed some very simple rules which have served me well throughout my military service:

- Always put the care and well-being of your soldiers before self.
- Great things can be accomplished if you worry little about who gets the credit.
- Stand firm for what you believe to be right—even it's not popular.

"I am convinced that one has experienced a successful life when he can look back upon it with the sure knowledge he would change very little."

Lieutenant General Charles Roadman, U.S. Air Force (Ret.)
Former USAF Surgeon General

"Integrity first, service before self, and excellence in all things we do: these core values serve as our road map and set the standards for our behavior. They serve to remind us of the importance of the profession we have chosen, the oath we have taken, and the demands placed upon us as members of the profession at arms. These values are for life, not just for working hours."

General Charles T. Robertson, Jr., U.S. Air Force

"Throughout my life, I've really only been guided by two simple leadership principles: First, in whatever you do and whatever you touch, leave it better than you found it. I don't stay awake at night worried that I haven't changed the world or that I've only influenced a small number of issues of people. I simply do my best to leave what I can affect better than it was when I found it. I draw hope from the notion that the people I influence may do the same.

Second, *take time to care for* your fellow man. It's not the same as *take care of* your fellow man, and its not easy in this hectic lifestyle we lead. Put yourself in his shoes, understand his problems, show genuine interest, listen, and above all, take time for his concerns. It takes personal involvement and time. It takes thought and emotion. And, it's always enriching.

"All senior leaders, as they mature, begin to wonder what value they've added to their organization and their people. I take great solace that, in the end, I'll know that I truly did my best to care for and understand the people and issues I could touch, and that I left them better than I found them."

General Michael E. Ryan
U.S. Air Force

"I would have to agree with my father, General John D. Ryan, the Air Force's seventh Chief of Staff, that integrity is our most important responsibility. In a policy letter he wrote for his commanders, he stated that, 'Commanders are dependent on the integrity of those reporting to them in every decision they make. Integrity can be ordered, but it can only be achieved by encouragement and example.' I believe his message is as meaningful today as it was when he wrote it, more than 25 years ago. And, as one of the Air Force's core values, integrity helps inspire the trust which provides the unbreakable bond that unifies our force."

Captain Walter M. Schirra, Jr.
U.S. Navy (Ret.)
Mercury, Gemini, and Apollo Astronaut

"I believe that success comes from being a good team leader. My U.S. Navy career was enhanced due to my remembering advice from a Chief Petty Officer who said, 'You midshipmen, now or after becoming officers, whenever in doubt or when lacking data remember to consult your chief.' I have on many occasions, and I say 'Hail to the chiefs!' The success of the NASA team who sent man to the moon is the result of over 300,000 members in real time working together. We went to the moon and back!"

General Peter J. Schoomaker
U.S. Army (Ret.)
Former CINC USSOCOM

1. Be yourself...above all else.
2. Be positive...your attitude directly affects the ability of your people to accomplish tasks they may not think they are capable of accomplishing.
3. Be conscious of others, make everyone feel important—they are.
4. Be going somewhere...have a vision and supporting goals.

Make sure your organization is aligned with this vision.
5. Play as hard as you can, and the score will take care of itself.
6. Don't worry about who gets credit...the whole team wins.
7. Share your power and authority with others. Push responsibilities down to the lowest level and underwrite honest mistakes.

General H. Norman Schwarzkopf
U.S. Army (Ret.)
Former CINC, Desert Shield/Storm

"Always try to do your very best, but recognize that success is not what you gain for yourself, but what you do for others. Character is far more important than competence. Therefore, one must always pick the harder right over the easier wrong. When the tough decision must be made, do what's right. It won't always be popular, but if you live your life with absolute integrity, you will learn that the rewards of moral character come from character itself. Do what's right, and remember you can't help someone up a hill without getting closer to the top yourself."

Major General Patrick Sculley
U.S. Army

"I believe that leaders are created rather than born, and that it is the sum total of life's experience that molds the leader. Thus, the experiences gained throughout life have great impact on one's leadership ability. It is important to have a broad perspective of the human condition. I learned as much about leadership as a dishwasher, Convenient Food Mart manager, and minor professional football player as I did in various leadership laboratories of the military. It was these experiences that created a solid respect for the dignity of all people which guided my subsequent military career.

"Vicarious experience is important to the development of the leader. One can gain leadership perspectives by observing the actions of others in leadership positions. I have witnessed great leadership and poor leadership. It is possible that the poor leaders have created more lasting impact by engendering an abiding desire not to emulate them.

"The *sine qua non* of good leadership is setting the right example in all endeavors. It entails technical and tactical knowledge; but more important, it means evidencing a constancy of purpose and a system of values. Great leaders always strive to do the 'right thing,' even at their own expense. When I reflect on the great leaders I have known, I realize that they all were 'easy reads.' I knew how they would respond to every opportunity and challenge, and that the response would always be consistent with their value system. They were not inflexible, nor were they easily discouraged. When encountering an obstacle, they were capable of adjusting their azimuth to be consistent with their values and approaching their goal from a different direction. They also were very resilient. Dark clouds always had a silver lining, and every challenge also presented opportunity."

General John Shalikashvili
U.S. Army (Ret.)
Former Chairman, Joint Chiefs of Staff

"During my first assignment as a young Lieutenant, a superb NCO taught me three basic tenets of leadership—principles that have served me well for 39 years.

"The first is *competence*. One cannot be a leader without the intense discipline of forging professional competence. The second is *compassion*—caring for America's sons and daughters whose lives are in the hands of our leaders. This philosophy includes challenging subordinates to achieve high standards of excellence, thereby helping them gain confidence. Last, and perhaps most important, is *character*. There is no substitute for doing what is right and for holding the moral and ethical high ground."

General Hugh Shelton
U.S. Army

"The following philosophy has served me well for 33 years of service in our Armed Forces. First, if we empower people to do what is legally, ethically, and morally right, there is absolutely no limit to what we can accomplish. Leaders must look to their people and focus on the good. Secondly, leaders must create an environment where people can be all they can be. Lastly, you must treat others as you would have them treat you. A leader must have compassion—a basic respect for the dignity of each individual. This is a simple restatement of the Golden Rule—but it is a critical issue."

Major General John Singlaub
U.S. Army (Ret.)

"I frequently speak to ROTC cadets and young officers. I tell them very frankly that they must live a life with integrity. If they do not have integrity and do not believe in telling the truth, then they are not being completely honest with themselves, and the military does not need them.

"This is an essential component for a successful military career. They must be trustworthy; and they cannot, under any circumstance, give a false statement. That can lead to the loss of lives and wrong decisions. Therefore, the most important quality for professional officers, for leaders, is integrity.

"We have problems today because the educators in the 1960s suggested that there was no standard of behavior or ethic to adhere to. Students were taught to do what was best for themselves and what felt good. I believe this is an invitation for disaster. The United States is 'reaping the harvest' of this concept of the 'ME' generation. We cannot have a civilization and an efficient government if we have people whose attitude and behavior reflect this concept. Integrity is the key to success and significance!"

Brigadier General James Spivey
U.S. Army Reserves
Southwestern Baptist Theological Seminary

"How do we measure success? Some people esteem status; others value possessions; still others focus on accomplishments. Status, possessions and accomplishments: are these really definitive yardsticks for assessing success?

"'No,' our hearts whisper, hinting that ultimately these are empty, even deceitful standards. They lead us to compare ourselves with other people who, in turn, vainly compare themselves with us; so these are uncertain and unreliable. Rather than focusing on the real value of the true person, they measure superficial things such as position and performance. Remember, rank loses its luster; the flush of victory subsides; and the reins of power inevitably pass to a new generation. People soon forget how once they were impressed by your position, your power, your possessions. In the long run, they remember you for who you are, for how you treat them, and for how wisely you use your position and power. In short, they admire strength of character as defined by service, respect, and integrity. These three qualities mark the difference between success and significance.

"First the truly significant leader does not chase personal success; he empowers others to succeed and cares for them before himself. To lead, he knows he must first serve.

"Second, he avoids using people as means to an end, but treats everyone with respect because of their inherent human dignity. So, he does not use people and cherish things; he uses things and cherishes people. He puts people before accomplishments, even before organizational success. He realizes that if he takes care of people, they will take care of the organization. He does unto others as he would have others do unto him.

"Third, character is measured ultimately by integrity. More than telling the truth, this goes beyond honesty. More than doing the right thing, this goes beyond propriety. More than living by one's own set of core values, this goes beyond personal identity. Integrity is being true to what God calls us to be and do, not just in speech but also in action. When all the trappings of success are stripped away—and someday this will happen to us all—what remains? It is the investment we have made in other people and the testimony of our obedience to God. Success fades, but character endures. The pathway from success to significance is measured by our selfless service, our respect for others, and our personal integrity."

General Gordon Sullivan
U.S. Army (Ret.)
Former Chairman, Joint Chiefs of Staff

"Often, I am asked for advice by young leaders. I try to keep my focus clear for them just as I would have wanted it at their age:
- When you are a leader, you are responsible.
- Treat people with dignity and respect.
- Always do the best job you can.
- Selfless service means selfless service.
- Be loyal to your troops and your nation—this is not easy.
- Enjoy life."

General John Tilelli, Jr.
U.S. Army (Ret.)
Former CINC, United Nations Command

"Each and every day, resolve to do your best. The foundation for sustained, high quality performance is internalization of bedrock values like honor, duty, courage, respect, loyalty, and service. These simple guideposts ensure you choose the harder right over the easier wrong. They ensure you care for others before self. They ensure you commit to excellence in assigned tasks. They ensure you provide a climate where subordinates develop competence and achieve their potential without fear of making mistakes. In the final analysis, leaders who subscribe to these values understand with absolute clarity that any success they achieve is more a result of their team's efforts rather than their own. Thirty-seven years of service observing superb Soldiers, Sailors, Airmen, Marines, and family members in the U.S., Vietnam, Germany, the Gulf War, and Korea have convinced me of the value of this philosophy."

Major General Harold L. Timboe, U.S. Army

"As a physician and medical leader, it has been my life's calling to care for Army families. Servant leadership as epitomized in the life and words of Jesus best describes the hallmark of a successful leader. I have found four attributes essential to the servant leader.

"First, a belief from the heart of the calling to the mission. Only through a true belief in the importance and significance of what you are doing can you have a real dedication to duty and a sense of commitment to achieving success. Second, a servant leader must genuinely care for others and those they serve.

"Third, a leader must display a high level of competence in their area of expertise. This is attained through a lifetime of learning, and this competence must be continually improved. Fourth, character to know what is right and do the right thing even when no one is looking—except God. Leaders must have the character expected of the high calling of our profession. My prayer is that during my positions of authority I have been a role model and mentor who has sufficiently shown the way in believing, caring, competence, and character, such that when God calls me to rest He will include the phrase: 'Well done thou good and faithful servant, be thou at peace.'

"Living that code can only come from a reliance on God's strength and knowing that I am seeking and am in His will doing what He has called me to do. Perhaps this is best exemplified in Paul's attitude expressed to the Galatians: 'I am crucified with Christ, nevertheless I live, but not I, Christ lives in me, and the life which I now live in the flesh I live by the faith of the Son of God, who loved me and gave himself for me.' This creed sustains me in living out the code of servant leadership.

"Living a life of significance comes from knowing the purpose for which you were created and consistently using your God-given potential to turn success into significance. I seek to love God and enjoy Him forever as He conforms us to the image of His Son. As St. Francis of Assisi said, 'Preach always, and sometimes use words.' Significance comes from having a godly impact on the hearts and lives of others through your words and actions."

Major General Robert Van Antwerp, U.S. Army

"BE A SERVANT LEADER. This is the way the Leader of leaders, Jesus Christ, led. He washed feet, He noticed when hurting people touched His robe or sought Him for healing—physical, emotional, or spiritual. He was never too busy for His people; they were His main concern. He died for them. There is no job beneath the dignity of a servant leader. He leads by example.

"SEEK WISE COUNSEL BUT THINK INDEPENDENTLY. The best leaders are independent thinkers who trust their instincts and intuition but seek wise counsel.

"PROVIDE INSPIRATION. Leaders must inspire their people to go beyond that which they think is possible. When an inspiring leader turns around, he finds he has people following him wherever he goes, no matter how difficult the challenge.

"BE CALM AND RESILIENT. The great leaders are calm in crisis and resilient in adversity and disappointment. They have allowed trouble and tribulation to build character. If you stay in top spiritual and physical shape, you will withstand the emotional strain of crisis. God is large and in charge, and He has a plan. Adversity is the best character builder and you can believe that God knows that. Learn the lessons that come from going through adversity well."

General William Westmoreland
U.S. Army (Ret.)
Commander (MACV) 1964-68,
USA Chief of Staff 1968-72, AUS

"If I were to offer advice about my creed or code of conduct for life I would recommend the Golden Rule: 'Do unto others what you would have them do unto you.' This is basic to achieving success and significance."

Major General Jerry E. White
U.S. Air Force (Ret.)
President, The Navigators

"My personal code of conduct is found in Jesus' Sermon on the Mount. 'But seek first the kingdom of God and His righteousness, and all these things shall be added to you' (Matthew 6:33 NKJ). If God is first in life, everything else comes together. When you act with righteousness, justice, and integrity, personally and toward others, then relationships and service to others have the ring of truth and combat selfishness and prideful competition. For me, success in a worldly sense is up to God. If success comes, I must simply use my God-given gifts and opportunities to serve well and to give credit to the many—God, first, of course—who have helped along the way. Then significance comes from realizing that only people count—not things or accomplishments. I have come to recognize that my true significance resides in my personal relationship to Jesus Christ and the way that I live out that relationship day-by-day in my leadership, my family, and my personal life."

General Johnnie E. Wilson
U.S. Army (Ret.)
Former Commander, United States Army Materiel Command

"I grew up in a family of 12 children and what I remember most about my family is that we always worked together. We had to share our shoes, shirts, and trousers. But we also shared a love and respect for each other. There was always this sense of 'Do what's right and we'll make it.' Religion is very important to me, and faith has given me strength throughout my life. I like to tell young people that we're all different. Some of us are tall, some are short, some are of a different color, but we are one as Americans. We must learn to respect each other, our classmates, our teachers, our elders, our parents, and we will succeed as a nation. I believe in America. I believe we can be a better America."

Major General James W. Wurman, U.S. Army (Ret.)

"I started my military career in the U.S. Navy during the Korean War, serving as an enlisted sailor for two years. As a young sailor, I was fascinated by the leadership styles of my leaders. I did not realize how significantly I was impressed in those early days. As I progressed through the ranks in the Army, I tried to adopt the good leadership traits and cast aside negative methods.

"Leadership is centered around people and respect. If a leader tries to lead, keeping people as the core, chances are that he or she can be successful. Respect is required and can be attained by using the following basic skills: First, treat people as you would like to be treated. Secondly, speak to people in the same manner in which you desire to be addressed. Last, but not least, profanity is not necessary.

"When a leader has the respect of subordinates, tough decisions can be handled easily because the leader has the confidence of the subordinates."

Brigadier General Charles E. Yeager, U.S. Air Force (Ret.)

First pilot to break the speed of sound.

"By the time I left my home in West Virginia at age 18, I think that I had been taught, by my parents, everything that made me what I am today. The phrase 'duty to God and country' was paramount in our life. Our whole life was lived at face value: your expression reflected what you thought. Duty was why I flew in combat, why I did dangerous research flying, and why I was in command of the best units in the Air Force. If more people put a little duty, instead of money and fame in their life today, I think this would be a much better world."

Vice Admiral James Zimble U.S. Navy (Ret.)

Former USN Surgeon General
President, Uniformed Services University of the
Health Sciences

"Whenever asked by an individual for advice regarding the "best job" to seek for career advancement, my response is that the "best job" is the one he or she currently occupies. Doing the very best in the job at hand should lead to career advancement. And doing the best in the job includes giving credit to others for successful accomplishments and accepting responsibility for failures. In my book, that's real leadership!"

PART III
Ex-POWs

"He has sent me to bind up the brokenhearted, to proclaim freedom for the captives and release for the prisoners. . ."
(Is. 61:1).

Lieutenant Colonel Carey E. Ashcraft, U.S. Army (Ret.)
Ex-POW, WWII, Germany

"My advice to others is: Never stop trying, continue to reach ahead and higher. If someone else can do something, I believe that I can learn to do it also. Always be honest, have faith in God, let prayer be part of your daily life. Wisdom is the principal thing, therefore get wisdom and receive understanding.

"When my father received the telegram stating that I was missing in action, he prayed. That night the Lord revealed to him in a dream that I was captured and how. I would also like to encourage others to read daily from the Psalms and Proverbs."

William E. Bearisto
Ex-POW, WWII, Germany
National Commander
AX-POWs, 1993-94

"I was a prisoner of war captured in Germany in December of 1944 at the 'Battle of the Bulge.' At the age of 19, I had already served in four major campaigns.

When captured, I lost my freedom. My concern and thoughts about my future and what would happen to me caused great duress. I did not know if I would live or die. Food was very scarce. I lost 60 pounds during my imprisonment.

I frequently prayed that I would survive and live to see my family again. My faith in God helped me to carry on. I looked forward to the time when I would be free again and return home to my family.

After joining the American Ex-Prisoners of War Association, I worked through the ranks to become the National Commander. This was a very rewarding experience. Later I became the President of the American Ex-Prisoner Of War Service Foundation.

I was blessed with a successful business, a great family, and a wife who truly cared. Every day I give thanks to God for allowing me to be free in the greatest country in the world, the United States of America!"

Lieutenant Colonel Robert W. Bieber
Ex-POW, WWII, Germany

"I was an aircraft commander on a B-24 flying with the 8th Air Force out of England. On the 17th of January, 1945, our aircraft took a direct hit from an 88-mm anti-aircraft gun over Harburg, Germany. Three of us were still in the B-24 when it exploded.

"I regained consciousness in a small part of the remaining cockpit, which was hurtling toward the ground. I pushed myself clear of the wreckage and pulled my ripcord. When the chute opened, I was no higher than 1000 feet. I saw pieces of my aircraft falling all around me. Even though my parachute was damaged by the fire, I survived the landing.

"I couldn't stand up or walk and spent one week in a German hospital until I could. Then I was sent to an interrogation camp and several POW camps, and on a forced march from Nuremberg to Mooseberg, Stalag Luft VIIA. I was liberated in early May by General Patton's 3rd Army.

"I learned how to pray on the 17th of January, 1945. My prayer was short, 'Father in heaven, thank you.' I did a lot of praying while a POW. Most of my prayers were asking for protection from the harm all around us, and then thanking God for survival. My experience, being in the aircraft when it exploded and surviving months as a POW, taught me two things.

"First, I learned that God is alive and in His heaven. He is good, He listens, and He answers. Second, when I ask Him for help, I must expect Him to help. I must not doubt that my prayers will be answered. This positive attitude is very important when praying. I must 'enthusiastically believe' my prayers will be answered. 'Ask, and it shall be given to you; seek, and you shall find; knock, and it shall be opened to you.' (Matthew 7:7)

"I have applied these two lessons to my life, ever since 1945. Through good times and bad, in good health and with two bouts with cancer, and during unbelievably difficult circumstances, they have never failed me!"

Vernon Brooks
Ex-POW, WWII, Germany

"In February, 1942, I was called to defend my country. I received my training at Fort Lewis, Washington, and then went on to Boston and from there I shipped to France.

"I was captured in 1945 in France by the Germans. We moved a lot, never staying in one place for any length of time. They moved us in boxcars the Germans called 40 and 8—which meant that they would hold 40 men or 8 horses. Food was scarce. We usually got one potato each day and sometimes a stale slab of bread. After being held prisoner for four months, I was liberated by my fellow countrymen. During the time I was held prisoner, I asked the Lord several times to get me home safely. My prayers were answered.

"My mother gave me a small Bible when I left home for basic training. I carried it with me at all times. My oldest grandson asked for the Bible when he graduated from high school so he could take it to college with him. When I gave it to him, he remarked, 'Grandpa, it got you through the war and home safely. I will carry it to college to help me on my way.'

"Upon my release from the Army, I started farming and spent my life tilling the soil. It seemed like the most peaceful occupation. I thank the Lord that I made it through the war and am still here with my family."

Colonel William G. Byrns
U.S. Air Force (Ret.)
Ex-POW, Vietnam

"The military trains us mentally and physically to be leaders. It truly is the best training in the world. The key to successful leadership is the development of the spiritual part of our being. I have noticed, over my 30 years of service, that the most outstanding leaders I have met have a deep faith in God. Some of those leaders have had to lead under extremely adverse conditions such as in combat and in a prisoner of war situation. The North Vietnamese were able to eventually weaken us mentally and physically but could not weaken us spiritually. Without Jesus Christ as my Lord and Savior, I could not have made it. The core values of integrity, service, and excellence are critical to leadership and can be absolute when we are mentally, physically and spiritually developed as leaders. The combination then produces character. Character is doing the RIGHT THING when no one else, except God, is looking."

Colonel Fred V. Cherry
U.S. Air Force (Ret.)
Ex-POW, Vietnam

"My seven and a half years as a prisoner of war (POW) in North Vietnam will always have an impact on my life. I survived the pain, torture, isolation, loneliness, and hopelessness through my faith in God, family, country, fellow prisoners, and self. I relied on my Christian faith to get me through the toughest times. I was thankful for my Christian upbringing and the values which I had been taught by my family, elders, and teachers. When all hope seemed to fade and creep away, my faith would grasp the fading hope and reel it back within my reach. Without the sound values deeply imbedded in me, my performance as an American fighting man in the hands of the enemy would have been miserable and so would my ability to face myself in a mirror today.

"We must continue to teach our young people the sound values which have been the foundation for all great people and nations. Our youth are our future, and the survival of our nation will depend on their leadership. We must develop leaders with unwavering character, integrity, honesty, moral character, and love. Young Americans—have faith, set your goals high, and aspire to be the best that you can be. Build your foundation on the values that have made great men, women, and nations."

Howard Chrisco
Ex-POW, WWII, Bataan

"I am a humble World War II soldier who experienced the atrocious and brutal acts committed against the United States forces during the 'Death March' in the Philippines. I was a prisoner for 15 months before escaping and living with Filipino guerrillas for ten months. Through short-wave radio, we made contact with the submarine, Crevalle, which returned me to Australia.

"My survival as a prisoner was only possible because of my strong will to live and my personal faith in God. Still, at times, I wasn't sure I would make it. These experiences strengthened my faith in God; and today, I often find myself thanking Him for watching over me and caring for me.

"My wartime experiences certainly taught me how precious life is and impacted my living. I like to set goals and work until those goals are accomplished. I believe that honesty and treatment of my fellow man as I want to be treated, are important attributes to honor. Because of my experiences, I have a very positive outlook on life. God has been good to me, and I am grateful for the many years of health and happiness with my wife of 51 years and our two sons and their families."

Fred P. Dallas
Ex-POW, WWII, Germany
National Director, AX-POWs

"I grew up on a farm deep in the Mississippi farm country. We were a large family of eight children. Our mother and father taught us the importance of God, country, and family. I would not have survived the horrors of WWII without God by my side and the strong desire to be reunited with my loved ones. He was my strength during the time I spent as a prisoner of war in a forced labor camp in the coldest winter in Europe in 50 years. We were beaten, starved, and forced to work in weather below zero. Some of my fellow POWs froze to death, others starved to death. My strength in God and my determination are what brought me back home.

"Always have an abiding faith in God and be determined in all your endeavors, remember freedom is not free—ask any ex-POW. I hope our future generations will remember we fought for their freedom and we must always maintain a strong military."

Irving M. Day, Jr.
Ex-POW, WWII, Germany

"I must have missed the lecture on 'Bail-out Procedure.' On April 11, 1944, I found myself confronted with the necessity of leaving my burning B-24 'Liberator' bomber, which had been critically damaged by flak over Germany. I was convinced that I could not leave through that small, nose-wheel hatch. After some vacillation, I decided that my bride would want me to, at least, try to exit. I stood beside that hole in the floor, hesitating; the next thing I knew I was falling in space. To this day, I am convinced that it was the hand of God that pushed me out of that airplane. It had to be Him, as Marin was definitely not present to assist me; only the thought of her! I discovered later that I bumped my head as I fell, a persistent trauma, but a small cost for life.

"When an airplane was shot down over enemy territory prior to D-Day, it was a foregone conclusion that the occupants were destined to be either POW or KIA. To this day, I still do not know why I was spared, but I thank God daily for His kindness in allowing me to become a Prisoner of War (and, more importantly, an ex-POW)! I do not brag that God protected me, but I am completely mystified.

"The loss of one's freedom, devastating though it may seem at the time, is a temporary condition. However, the punishment of incarceration without crime for just doing one's duty is for most individuals a psyche-scarring experience. It is difficult for such subjects to provide leadership, or respond to the leadership of peers. The ex-POW is prone to consider his cup to be half-empty, instead of still half-full. He dwells upon reasons why a project might fail, whereas a non-POW would consider reasons for success.

"Whether he recognizes these truths, the ex-POW needs God's

help and the reassurance of God's love, even though that love has already been demonstrated through His great gift of life. By admitting our frailty and striving with prayer to rise above it, we can hope to inspire our children and grandchildren to respect us and to frequently rely on God in their lives."

Jeremiah Denton
RADM, USN, (Ret.), Ex-POW, Vietnam,
Former Senator, Alabama

"My creed for life is the Apostles' Creed. My code of conduct is derived from the Ten Commandments and Jesus' command to 'love God, and your neighbor as you love yourself.'

"As an American naval officer, I derived motivation to serve my nation because of my love for my country. I also believe that Americans have a special justification to love their country derived from a love of God.

"America was founded as 'one nation under God.' Our founding fathers deliberately based their experiment in democracy upon the premise that the compassion and the self-discipline required for the success of a democracy can only come from citizens who believe strongly in God.

"Christianity embodies the belief that the ultimate success is heaven, and that it can only be attained in loving your neighbor as you love yourself. This belief provides compassion and self-discipline, which are the keys to our thesis and to our success.

"Due to our nation's founding premise, I found it easy to serve in a profession that protected our land. My generation helped to protect and ensure the survival of our nation against Fascism and Soviet Communism. Now our greatest enemy is the threat that would do away with America's belief in the founding premise, its founding thesis.

"If we continue to increase our forgetfulness of God's ultimate significance, then America will not survive. I strive for the ultimate significant success—heaven—by loving and serving God, country, and family."

C. Earl Derrington, Jr.
Ex-POW, WWII, Germany
National Commander, AX-POWs 1983-84

"Every facet of one's life is molded by the events encountered along the way. My formative years began with a loving mother, father, and brother. Church was a very important issue in my family. Consequently, when I became a prisoner of war in Germany in 1944, it was my faith and strong bond of love within my family that sustained me.

"As an adult, I find that the more I give of my time and of myself in helping others, the more enriched my life becomes. My advice for young people of today is to preserve the family, strengthen their spiritual faith, and keep their commitment to God, family, and country."

Carl E. Edwards
Ex-POW, WWII, Germany

"It was at the command of my CO that I laid down my weapon and surrendered to the enemy in WWII. While it is important to lead, it is equally important to follow a command. That is the only reason I am alive today.

"When God gives an order from His Word, it is in our best interest to follow this order. When we surrender to the enemy, we give up all of our earthly freedoms, but he cannot take away our faith in God.

"My code of conduct is READ GOD'S WORD, PRAY FOR KNOWLEDGE, then apply it to our daily walk with humility."

Colonel Lee Ellis
U.S. Air Force (Ret.)
Ex-POW, Vietnam

"As a POW, I tried to live by the American Fighting Man's Code of Conduct. In the process, I learned many things that have helped me in my struggle to live a life that honors God and blesses my fellow man.

1. Live by principles and values. The Bible offers truths that

have stood the test of time and can guide you in relationships, finances, business, and literally every area of your life.

2. Have the courage (faith) to do what is right even when it is difficult or unpopular. It's the price of integrity, and our POW leaders paid it through their personal sacrifice.

3. Be yourself. You are a unique creation so don't compare yourself to someone else. Focus on your talents and passions and use them to accomplish your life purpose/mission.

4. Think about the long term goal and beware of taking the easy way out. My five and a half years in the camps taught me the value of commitment and persistence.

5. Take care of your people. Avoid the natural urge to further your own self interest at the expense of others—be a giver, not a taker.

6. Face up to your weaknesses and learn about your blind spots. In the camps, we had lots of time to take inventory and get feedback. When you admit you don't have it all together, God can do a great work in your life."

Wendell Fetters
Ex-POW, WWII, Germany

"On December 23, 1944, we were shot down during the Battle of the Bulge. We were scheduled to be sent to Barth, which originally was a POW camp for Air Force officers. Later in the war it was for non-commissioned officers as well.

"When our train, which contained 50-60 Army Air Force personnel, was shot up in the rail yards of Berlin, we were 'dumped' off at Stalag 3A at Luckenwald, Germany. It was a pretty dismal place. We all had lice, bedbugs, and sand fleas for company.

"The British compound was to the west; the Russian compound to the east. We were not fed well! The Russians, it appeared, were fed even less. The problem, the Germans told us, was that our Red Cross parcels came out of Switzerland and our Air Force had bombed all the rail yards, bridges and shot up the trucks on the roads so no parcels got through to the POWs. That was probably true, but as a result we were fed a slice of what we referred to as 'sawdust' black bread, and one or two small potatoes a day and sometimes a cup of soup with questionable ingredients.

"Our rations, as well as the Russians', were based on the daily 'headcount.' During the daily head count, because food was so important, the Russians would hold up their dead as long as it was possible, just to get their extra rations. Sounds gruesome, but for survival it was all important.

"When we were liberated by the Russian army, it was a joyful occasion. Everyone was happy and the fences were torn down so all the prisoners intermingled. A Russian, probably an officer, wearing brown trousers with a red stripe down the leg, took me by the arm and steered me into the nearest barracks. It was dark, dank, and bug infested. At the north end of the building in all its glory, was a beautiful statue of Jesus in a garden-like setting. It was complete with angels painted in the background. I could hardly believe my eyes! I was awestruck. Here in the midst of squalor and despair was the work of what we had been led to believe were 'godless' Russians. It proved to me that even in Communism, Christ was ever present!"

Stephen Fitzgerald
Ex-POW, WWII, Germany

"The following is what impelled me, through my life, to distinguish between success and the appreciation of the significance of Jesus Christ.

"I attended a rather strict ROTC military high school where I won some academic awards and a medal for excellence in military science and tactics. Looking back, I believe I was an arrogant, self-confident know-it-all until I came very close to dying from a ruptured appendix during a field maneuver far from a hospital.

"Graduating from high school in 1944 at age 18, I volunteered for immediate induction into the army infantry, the 'Queen of Battle.' I had hoped to go to Officer's Candidate School; and after combat, apply for language school; and thereafter, enter into military intelligence training. However, the Battle of the Bulge broke out in Europe in December 1944, and we were taken out of incomplete basic training with orders to go to Europe.

"I was given a two-day 'Delay in Route' to spend time at home on Christmas Eve and Christmas Day. Being at boot camp was a relief in a sense because my beloved mother, an Irish Catholic of the old school, insisted on obeying not only the Ten Commandments but every rule and regulation of the church. She insisted on attending Mass on Christmas Day even though I told her I had a lot of sleep to catch up on.

"A month or so later, I was captured and forced to march across freezing central Europe with very little to eat and sleeping mostly in the open. Carrying our sick and wounded was another major burden.

"One of my feet became infected and so swollen that it was

twice its normal size. Surgery and possible amputation was to be done on my foot for which there was no anesthetic. While being held down on a dirty mattress in a filthy prison camp infirmary by five men, I could only move my head. Looking down I saw a little cloth picture of Jesus that my mother had sewn on my long underwear over my heart. I prayed very earnestly that I would not lose my foot. The American paratrooper doctor told me that he was not at all sure that he could save the foot, but I am sure that it was the Lord Jesus Christ who saved it. To this day, my feet are perfect and I enjoy good health."

Major William L. Fornes
U.S. Air Force (Ret.)
Ex-POW Korea

"I think the best advice anyone has given about becoming a POW is the advice of Congressman Sam Johnson in the video *Echos of Captivity:* 'Don't get captured.'

"If I was to give advice about my creed or code of conduct for life, this comes to mind: I believe our nation needs to get its priorities in line, not only the military but our society as a whole. For years we fought the 'cold war'; now we are fighting the drug war. I see the American public as self-serving and without resolve. As a result, we are undermining the principles our forefathers created for us and expected us to preserve. I am reminded of the verse of scripture engraved on the prisoner of war statue in Georgia, 'Turn you to the stronghold ye prisoners of hope.' (Zechariah 9:12). That's what we need to do. We need to turn once again to those principles that made America great."

Carl J. Fyler
Ex-POW, WWII, Germany

"During the war, I always took my crew to the base Protestant chapel for services. In combat, when a flak battery got a bead on my ship, I'd pray that I could get my crew back to England. Sometimes the whole sky was full of 'flak.' Once, two big shells tore up the right wing and killed two engines. The plane fell 21,000 feet. With the help of my co-pilot, we tipped the B-17 over on the left wing and flew sideways 500 miles at 100 feet. We destroyed two enemy planes sent out to 'get us.' We landed at an emergency field in England. At the VA when asked if I believed in God, I answered, yes. So much has happened to me; God must have saved me for a reason."

Bruce E. Hall
Ex-POW, WWII, Italy & Germany
National Director, AX-POWs,

"I was a private in the 45th Infantry Division, 157th Regiment, during WWII. I joined them as a replacement just prior to landing at Salerno, Italy, on September 9th, 1943.

"I was assigned to the heavy mortar platoon of Company H.

My best buddy (Bob) was assigned to a rifle company at the same time. Two days later as we were advancing, I saw a GI get shot and fall. I managed to get him and pull him back to cover. When I turned him over, I discovered, to my horror, that it was Bob. He looked up at me, said my name and died. To this day, I wonder why I survived when he and so many others did not. I know I was not the only one who prayed, so why did I make it? I had determined that I would make it regardless, but I was blessed to do so.

"We advanced as far as the mountains at Cassino where the winter line of the German army stopped us. Our Division was among those chosen to pull back to Naples to regroup for the landings at Anzio on January 19th, 1944. I was there one month before being captured along with most of my battalion.

"My entire life prior to going into the Army had been positive. My parents and I were active in church. I was also active in YMCA activities. It was this positive heritage that sustained me through the fierce fighting and my 15 months as a POW. I managed to escape in early April, 1945. I weighed 98 pounds when I finally reached the American lines. The faith that had been instilled in me during my childhood enabled me to know that I could and would survive. Throughout my life, I have tried to lead a life of helping others as a pharmacist, father, and leader with the American Ex-Prisoner of War Association."

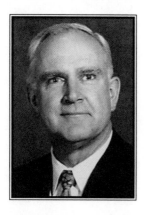

Commander Porter A. Halyburton
U.S. Navy (Ret.)
Ex-POW, Vietnam

"All through the seven and a half years of imprisonment in North Vietnam, my Christian faith was a constant source of great strength and comfort. I knew that this was something that my captors could never take away from me; but had they been able to destroy that faith, I do not think that I would have survived with any sense of integrity or honor. The struggle to live an honorable life and to find meaning in that life, no matter how miserable the circumstances, was the most important thing I could do.

"Over time I developed what I refer to as a Life Statement. It is as follows: I wish, at the instant of my death, to be able to look back upon a full and fruitful Christian life, lived as an honest man who has constantly striven to improve himself and the world in which he lives, and to die forgiven by God, with a clear conscience, the love and respect of my family and friends, and the peace of the Lord in my soul."

John E. Hanson
Ex-POW, WWII, Bataan, Philippines

"In the summer of 1942, following the fall of Bataan and Corregidor, I was held in the main Philippine prison camp at Cabanatuan with 5,000 other captives. There were 30–40 men dying each day from dysentery, malaria, and starvation. The Japanese guards despised us for having surrendered instead of fighting to the death and seemed to take great delight in making life as miserable as possible for the Americans under their control.

"The arithmetic of the situation indicated that all would be dead in a few months unless conditions improved. I did not think the Lord would answer prayers for more food or medicine, but I did pray for the strength to endure and survive.

"During those trying times, a creed evolved which has served me well in life:

1. Do the best you can with what you have.
2. If you are not in a position to help your neighbor, at least avoid harming him.
3. Value freedom. It becomes very precious once it has been lost.
4. Respect your body and mind. Feed each properly and do not abuse either.
5. Be kind to animals. This is very important. We are all creatures of God."

Gerald S. Harvey
Ex-POW, WWII, Germany

"As a child in Vacation Bible School, I learned this motto: 'I will do the best I can with what I have, where I am, for Jesus' sake, today.' This has stayed with me all my life—in the Air Force, as a prisoner of war, in school, in missionary service, in every part of my life.

"I also believe in setting goals ahead of where I am. As soon as I reach one, I set a new one. I have not reached all of my goals. However, when I fall short of the goal, I look for an open door, an opportunity, that God always has available.

"I believe that God will be with you through all of life until He calls you to be with Him."

Chief Warrant Officer Harland J. Hendrix U.S. Air Force (Ret.)
Ex-POW, WWII, Germany

"As a young boy at home, my name was mentioned out loud by my mother and father each evening near bedtime. They were kneeling at the piano bench praying for God's help and mercies to sustain me through life. Little did I know that this season of parental concern was preparation for events beyond my control in later life. When the Gestapo caught me evading in the area of the Pyrenees Mountains, survival from inhumane treatment came only through His mercies and my knowledge that someone at home (not only parents, but a loving and praying wife) was mentioning my name out loud to my Lord. Many death-threatening events were survived while thinking, 'Although I walk through the valley of the shadow of death, I fear no evil. For Thou art with me.' Many memory verses from the Bible, learned as a child, sustained me. They live in my memory today and are applied daily in decision-making, sensitivity to others, and thankfulness to my heavenly Father in the name of Jesus Christ. He is my refuge and my fortress. In Him will I trust.

"Throughout three careers, having learned somewhat about that which breaks a man's spirit, I have always asked God's wisdom in order to lead others to a faith in Him that embodies honesty, discipline, confidence, caring, teamwork, support, motivation, a positive attitude, and a complete understanding of His blessings. Jesus came that we might have life and have it more abundantly."

Wayne Hitchcock
National Commander,
AX-POWs 1997-98

"Having been a Boy Scout leader for several years, I believe strongly in the Scout Oath: 'On my honor I will do my best to do my duty to God and my country, and to obey the Scout Law; to help other people at all times; to keep myself physically strong, mentally awake, and morally straight.' What a wonderful world we would live in if everyone would subscribe to this. This puts God first and above all things.

"I would also recommend the memorization or frequent reading of the poem 'IF' by Rudyard Kipling. The poem ends with this well-known conclusion:

> If you can talk with crowds and keep your virtue,
>   Or walk with Kings—nor lose your common touch,
> If neither foes nor loving friends can hurt you,
>   If all men count with you, but none too much:
> If you can fill the unforgiving minute
>   With sixty seconds' worth of distance run,
> Yours is the Earth and everything that's in it,
>   And—which is more—you'll be a Man, my son!"

Colonel Roger D. Ingvalson
U.S. Air Force (Ret.)
Ex-POW, Vietnam

"All success is secular, all significance is spiritual. My goals in life changed after I was shot down and captured by the North Vietnamese just prior to my 40th birthday. It was on that day when Jesus Christ performed a miracle by sparing my life after ejection from my jet fighter at an extremely high speed. It was on that day that I became a Christian.

"My first 18 years of active duty in the USAF were spent attempting to achieve success in the secular world. Then, through my relationship with Christ, I realized that success was meaningless unless my life had a significance. Leadership by example became my motto as a military leader. My walk must equal my talk. I never gave an order without assuring that I could do it myself. After 26 years, I retired from the Air Force and formed a prison ministry. During the 15 years that I ministered to inmates, it was evident to me that unless I demonstrated a significance in my life, it was futile to try to see a change in inmates' lives."

Colonel Harold E. Johnson
U.S. Air Force (Ret.)
Ex-POW, Vietnam

"I grew up on a small farm in Iowa. My grandfather never learned to read or write, and my father only had a sixth grade education, but they were able to develop in me the spirit gained from hard work, a sense of values, a dedication to purpose, and a feeling of patriotism. My family weren't church going people, so I didn't have a development or appreciation of a religious faith until and during the six years of my captivity in North Vietnam. It was there I grew to understand why all men must find something greater than themselves to look up to and worship. My acceptance there of Jesus Christ as my Savior began a personal journey of enlightenment and guidance. The spiritual uplift gave me valuable insight and armed me with understanding. Excellent guidance gained is best demonstrated by one of my favorite Bible verses: 'Blessed is the man that walketh not in the counsel of the ungodly, nor standeth in the way of sinners, nor sitteth in the seat of the scornful. But his delight is in the law of the Lord; and in His law doth he meditate day and night' (Psalm 1.1).

"Life's lessons have taught me that leadership is of the spirit; management is of the mind. All people can be educated and trained to use the systems and methods available to organize and manage things. Only the strongly developed spirit in an individual can make them an effective leader of people. I have experienced it in myself and witnessed this spirit in the leadership of others which leads me to the conclusion that there are no great men—only great challenges to be met. Personal characteristics such as integrity, self-discipline, and emotional stability provide a person with the courage necessary to deal with all the challenges they encounter. God's grace massages the spirit of each individual in such a way that it highlights those characteristics of leadership necessary at any moment of trial and allows us to cope."

Colonel Sam Johnson
U.S. Air Force (Ret.)
Ex-Pow, Vietnam; Congressman, Texas

"I spent 29 years in the Air Force and was proud to answer my nation's call to service in Korea and Vietnam. The Air Force taught me the value of duty, honor, and country. And by nature, the military is committed to excellence and success. We send young men to battle to fight for our freedom and for democracy to win. We should all strive for success, but what is it that makes us significant?

"As a Prisoner of War in Vietnam for nearly seven years, I went through some difficult times. I spent 42 months in solitary confinement and 74 days in stocks. I wrote about my days in solitary confinement in my book, *Captive Warriors: A Vietnam POW's Story.*

"On the evening of my 74th day in stocks, I stared at the boarded-up window in my cell. It had been so long since I had seen the sky and the sun. My eyes blurred with tears, and at that moment, I felt suddenly finished. It was over; I couldn't fight any more. I remember thinking, as I fell asleep, exhausted and defeated that it would be okay if I never woke up again.

"Late that night, a typhoon tore through the city of Hanoi, ripping roofs off buildings and lashing the prison courtyard with wind and slicing rain. I awoke to the sounds of breaking glass and slamming window shutters. The floor of my cell was filled with water, and I huddled against the wall, as far away from the incoming rain as the leg stocks would allow me. The violence of the storm stirred something inside me, and I began to pray like I had never prayed before. Long after the storm subsided, I lay on my bunk, drenched from the rain, and strangely at peace in the darkness.

"I awoke the next morning to see my cell flooded with the first bright streaks of dawn. The storm had ripped the boards off my window, and for the first time in more than two months, sparkling rays of light danced a celebration in my tiny room. I had an overwhelming sense of the presence of God in that moment. He was with me, and He would be faithful. His fresh supply of mercy was pouring into my cell with all the reality of the sun's shining rays. I understood the Bible verse I learned as a child: 'His mercies are new every morning.' I was convinced that He would be sufficient for me; He would see me through.

"During my captivity, I realized that my significance comes from God. I am nothing without Him and while my military training prepared me well for my years of captivity, it was God who allowed my survival."

Major Kenneth Jones
U.S. Air Force (Ret.)
Ex-Pow, WWII, Germany

"On August 12, 1943, I was on my 17th combat mission as a ball-turret gunner when my B-17 and another plane from our squadron collided at 30,000 feet. Before the collision, our plane was attacked by ME-109's from the Herman Goering Fighter Squadron. I was wounded during the attack. Four of my crew members were also wounded. After our plane crashed, we were taken to a German military hospital. I remained in the hospital for about six weeks and was then transferred to Stalag 6G. I escaped but was recaptured and sent to Buchenwald to Dulag Luft. I spent five days in a boxcar that traveled to Stalag 17B in Kerms. In April 1945, Stalag 17B was evacuated, and we were forced marched from Kerms to Brauna, Austria. I was liberated by the 13th Army Division of the U.S. 3rd Army on May 2, 1945.

"If I was to offer my creed or code of conduct for life, I would offer the advice given to me by my grandparents. I was raised by my grandparents, the most loveable couple who lived by the motto, 'Be honest, truthful, and do unto others as you would have them do unto you, and God will take care of you and yours.' I have tried to live up to their motto and believe that I have, for God has most certainly taken care of me and mine."

Colonel George Juskalian
U.S. Army (Ret.)
Ex-POW, WWII, Germany

"At the end of WWII, I was privileged to be present when Chief of Staff of the Army, George C. Marshall, assembled his staff in his office in the Pentagon to thank them for their service and to bid them farewell. One phrase that he used in thanking his staff was their 'integrity of effort.' As I later reflected on those words, I realized that they were, in fact, a succinct statement of his own distinguished service to the nation. His staff had observed that quality in him and had responded in kind. From that time on, I adopted those words as my personal code of conduct because they embodied the values—honesty, loyalty, respect for others, courage, discipline, hard work—that I hold dear and which, in the eyes of my fellow man, I trust I have fulfilled."

J. Lawrence King
Ex-POW, World War II, Germany

"'Yea, Though I walk through the valley of the shadow of death, I will fear no evil; for thou art with me; thy rod and thy staff they comfort me' (Psalms 23:4).

"From the time of my birth, I was taught by example, words, song, and worship by my loving Christian parents. They not only taught me by words, but more importantly, by example. The words from Psalms 23:4 are just words until we read, understand, and live knowing the truth they teach us. My faith is grounded in knowing that Jesus Christ has paid the price of my sins. And from the words of the Psalms, I know that I'm never alone.

"In a trench in France during WWII, I renewed my trust and faith in God and promised to serve Him if I lived through the war and shortly thereafter as a POW—not a bargain, but a promise. So I serve Him in whatever way I can, for He is my leader and source of my life. God loves you, too."

John Klumpp
Ex-POW, WWII, Germany
National Junior Vice Commander, AX-POWs

"I, like many combat veterans, really don't understand why some came back and others did not. Six out of nine of my crew died from flak wounds and/or from crashing into a pine forest. I was one of the three who survived, and have given God credit for saving and guiding me for a purpose.

"Still, after 56 years, I do not know what that purpose is, but I have felt that a power greater than anything I have ever felt has given me guidance since then. I continue to strive to do what is right and honorable in hope that some day I accomplish what the Lord has in mind for me. As for my code of conduct, I still remember my mother telling me that anything worth doing is worth doing right."

Frank A. Kravetz
Ex-POW, WWII, Germany
National Director, AX-POWs

"Our youth need to know that freedom is not free! My captors could not deny me my prayers to God. I fashioned a set of Rosary Beads from a piece of string with which I prayed. My strong faith, along with love of country and love of family, was my source of strength for my survival."

Clarence K. "Swede" Larson
U.S. Air Force (Ret.)
Ex-POW, WWII, Bataan and Japan

"Having been a POW for nearly four years, many thoughts of the reasons for my survival come back to me from time to time. One thought was that I never gave up. My father often made a remark that I often think of to this day: 'It could be worse!' There were times during my captivity when I almost gave up, but never did.

"One night a group of men (including me) fell asleep. When I awoke because of artillery fire, I discovered that the men on my left and on my right were both dead. The thought came to me that someone was watching over me and that someone was God.

During many close calls with death, I always looked upwards and said, 'Thank you, God!'

"I have given numerous speeches in high schools and different organizations about my survival. When I am asked how I survived, I don't say anything. I simply point to the sky and they understand that it was God who watched over me.

"My final words are about our flag which I pull out of my pocket and wave back and forth saying, 'HONOR YOUR FLAG. IT SPELLS FREEDOM – YOURS AND MINE – AND IT COMES AT A TERRIBLE PRICE!'"

James H. McCahon, DVM
Ex-POW, WWII, Bataan & Japan

"My experiences as a survivor of the Bataan Campaign, three-and-one-half years of Japanese prison camps, and the sinking of two Hell Ships—the Oryoku Murm and the Enoura Muru—proved to me that these three essentials: faith, hope and charity, are indispensable to survival.

"One of my first memories as a child was being taught that God is everywhere and is aware of our every thought and deed. I believe that this ubiquitous God has taught us, by written word, the difference between right and wrong. This has been my guide through life. One must have an unyielding faith in God and have the courage to do what is right no matter what the temptations might be to do otherwise.

"One must never lose hope that the strength of God is a part of each individual and prayer will release that strength. To give up hope in life's efforts means failure. To give up hope as a Japanese prisoner of war meant death.

"There is a demand on each individual to share his fortune with others. No matter how difficult one's life may become, there is always someone less fortunate. Share and be prayerfully thankful for those who share with you when you are in need.

"This same philosophy is a guide for all of life's situations. It is essential for success in one's profession as well as any other aspect of life."

Senator John McCain, Arizona
U.S. Navy (Ret.), Ex-POW, Vietnam

"Soon after I became an involuntary guest of the Democratic Republic of Vietnam, my host tried to persuade me to make a tape recording in which I would denounce my country's cause. When I resisted, they entreated me to do so by promising me that no one would know of my disloyalty. I responded, 'But I would know.' Virtually all my comrades who shared my situation responded in the same way.

"There may be times in your life when the consequences of your devotion to duty are so dire that you will be tempted to abandon it. There may be times when truly only you will know. But you will resist. I know you will. I know this because I have seen how profoundly human strength is empowered by the standards of our traditions.

"I have watched men suffer the anguish of imprisonment, defy appalling human cruelty until further resistance is impossible, break for a moment and then recover inhuman strength to defy their enemies once more. All these things and more I have seen. I will go to my grave in gratitude to my Creator for allowing me to stand witness to such courage and honor."

Captain Eugene "Red" McDaniel, U.S. Navy (Ret.)
Ex-POW, Vietnam
President, American Defense Institute

"Success becomes significance when it fits into God's plan, when our accomplishments somehow further His kingdom here on earth. Often that kind of significant success is not seen as success when measured in human standards.

"All my life I have strived to be successful: to be a great athlete in high school and college, to get 'outstanding' on my naval officer fitness reports, to be a 'top gun' naval aviator, to be a tough resister in a Communist prison, to be commanding officer of an aircraft carrier, to rise to the top in military rank, to found a defense policy organization that would have an impact, and to establish a thriving small business in my retirement. When measured by human standards, I've 'succeeded' in those areas, and I have been duly rewarded by athletic scholarships, early selection for service rank, military awards and decorations for my performance as a POW, choice duty assignments, and the praise of men.

"However, those rewards have not been my greatest rewards. My experience as a POW in Vietnam helped me to begin to see the difference between success as measured by men and success as seen through the eyes of God. There were many times in my lonely cell when my victories were known only by me and God, and I found that those victories were profoundly more rewarding than the times I received a pat on the back from my fellow POWs or a military award upon my release. Since my return to freedom, the opportunities I've had to share with other people the love of God that sustained me during my captivity have been infinitely more precious than my chestful of military decorations. Writing my book, *Scars and Stripes,* as a testament to God's faithfulness during those dark days has brought satisfaction not paralleled by the satisfaction of good fitness reports and military commendations.

"And by far, the greatest rewards have come from times when I've done something simply because it was the right thing to do, when I've been criticized or even ostracized for taking an unpopular stand on causes which look like failures in the eyes of the world. Then, just as in my lonely cell, God knows and I know, and that is enough. My success has become significance."

Colonel Norman McDaniel
U.S. Air Force (Ret.)
Ex-POW, Vietnam

"Who am I? Why am I here? How should I live? Correct answers to these questions and a personal, positive response to them is the key to a successful and significant life.

"First, I realize that I am a creation of the One, True, Almighty, and Everlasting God: the God of the Universe, and the Father of my Lord and Savior, Jesus Christ. I realize that through Christ, I have a personal, living relationship with God that is everlasting.

"Second, I realize that my purpose in this mortal life is to establish and strengthen a personal relationship with God, and to fulfill the unique purpose for which He created me.

"Third, I should live by having and nurturing a right relationship with God by being a minister of His (in helping the poor, needy, sick, suffering, and those who do not know Him or have not accepted Him), and by doing all that I do to His glory. Also, I should live by giving my devotion and energy (in following priority) to God, family, country, others, and self, while sincerely trusting in the Holy Spirit to maintain the right balance and the right emphasis at the right time.

"I accepted Jesus Christ as my Lord and Savior 15 years before I was shot down over North Vietnam and captured in 1966 during the Vietnam War. I spent almost seven years as a POW. During those long, endless years of torture, deprivation, and uncertainty, I was no stranger to God. I prayed, trusted in Him, drew closer to Him during those trying, perilous times, and He sustained me.

"My sincere advice to every person is found in the Bible, in Proverbs 3:5-6 which says, 'Trust in the Lord with all thine heart; and lean not unto thine own understanding. In all thy ways acknowledge Him, and He shall direct thy paths.'

"I am persuaded that becoming aware of one's sinful condition, accepting Jesus Christ as your personal Savior, and then trusting in the Lord each day is the key to real and lasting significance!"

Willis A. Meier
Ex-POW, WWII, Germany

"During WWII I served as an engineer/gunner on a B-24 Bomber crew with the 702nd Squadron, 445th Bomb Group, 2nd Air Division of the 8th Air Force. We were shot down on September 27, 1944, over Kassel, Germany. I was badly wounded, burned, and disabled. We bailed out at 28,000 feet. I survived three prison camps. When liberated by Russian troops, I weighed only 118 pounds.

"My survival was based upon my attitude and determination. My daily prayer and the Lord's protection from the constant terrors, hardships, and starvation were my only means of coping.

"Many of my comrades were truly unrecognized heroes, who paid a terrible price for serving their country. Therefore, we must continue to live up to America's sacred obligation to those who fought with honor and did not return home from many foreign battlefields. They deserve to never be forgotten.

"Success in life is the result of honesty, integrity, caring, communication skills, leadership, knowledge, and expertise in our field of endeavor. Prepare for tomorrow, and being in the right place at the right time will take care of itself."

Major Paul J. Montague
U.S. Marine Corps (Ret.)
Ex-POW, Vietnam

"Your past makes you what you are; never hide from the past. The best way to heal one's self is to talk about your experiences, and not keep them within yourself. During my five years as a POW, I met Christ and Satan. I quickly learned that only with God in total control could I have peace within myself. Only by having God in total control could I be a leader and an example to others."

Colonel Herschel S. "Scotty"
Morgan, U.S. Air Force (Ret.)
Ex-POW, Vietnam

"On 3 April, 1965, I was shot down over North Vietnam and captured two days later. During the next 2,872 days, I learned many things about myself and also many valuable lessons. The first is the value of freedom. The key to surviving those difficult, and sometimes brutal, circumstances was faith in God, my country, my fellow POWs, and in myself. I gained this faith throughout my life by 'osmosis,' by soaking up the values taught by parents, family, church, school, Sunday school teachers, scout leaders, and those special people that we all have in our lives. We find that when we have nothing else, faith sustains us!

"I learned not to worry about those things over which I had no control. I learned to pray not, 'Why did you do this to me, Lord?' rather I learned to ask God to give me the wisdom to know what is right and the strength to do it even when no one is watching.

"I have found that a leader communicates what he expects, then gives his people the tools and the breathing room to get the job done. Finally, he gives his people credit for what they have done and rewards them with praise and promotions. Action, not words, gets the job done."

William E. "Sonny" Mottern
Ex-POW, WWII, Germany
National Commander, AX-POWs 1996-97

"During WWII, U.S. troops were the best equipped fighting men in the world. But the one vital element that enabled me to survive the war and POW camp was not GI issue. It was supplied by my father and mother. It was portable, took no space in my barracks bag and, being invisible, could not be confiscated by the enemy. It was my faith...my Christian upbringing. My faith became a mighty bulwark against the brutality, cold, hunger, forced marches, boxcar rides, and bombing I endured. Faith became my constant companion, my comfort against the inhumanity of my enemy.

I did not have to return it to the quartermaster when I was discharged. I brought it back home with me and relied on it to help raise my family, run a successful business, and to return to society some of the good fortune that has come my way...through faith."

Captain James A. Mulligan
U.S. Navy (Ret.)
Ex-POW, Vietnam

"I learned the importance of all human companionship while kept in solitary confinement for more than three and one-half years. I could remember nothing bad about anyone I had ever known and would have given anything to have just one of them with me.

"In my life, the word *commitment* is the operative word for all those things I believe in: marriage, family, God, country, etc. You make a commitment to what you believe in, and you stand by that commitment.

"The word *persistence* is my guideline to reach goals and objectives. Be persistent and never, never, never ever give up, and eventually you will achieve what you are seeking. Remember that, with God, all things are possible! So learn to pray!"

William B. Murray
Ex-POW, WWII, Germany

"On January 6, 1922, I was born into a religious family that had faith in God and tried to do things the Lord's way. In the 30s, due to drought, dust storms, and the depression, my family's faith was put to the test!

"I was married to Norma Jean Montgomery in May, 1942. During these 56 years, our faith and love have grown together.

"I joined the Army Air Corps as a private in September, 1942. In April 1944, on my 14th bombing raid over Germany, I was shot down and taken a prisoner of war for 13 months. My faith was extremely tested, not knowing what was in the future.

"I believe faith in God is what gives a person a meaningful and successful life."

Walter Pawlesh
Ex-POW, WWII, Austria
National Commander, AXPOW 73-74

"I feel we must always play the cards in life that God has dealt us. I may not know where my mission in life will take me or what God wants me to do, but I must try to make the right decisions. My faith is my main guide through life.

"I remember while I was a tailgunner on a B-17 Flying Fortress Bomber, I had a pattern that I followed before each mission. When the pilot would release the brakes of the plane, I would start saying the 'Lord's Prayer,' and I completed it before we lifted off the runway. The name of our bomber was 'Heaven Can Wait,' and it always lived up to its name, as it brought our crew of ten men back safely from the war. We were shot down and crashed landed, but all the crew was alive.

"I remember a story a POW friend of mine related to me. He would go to visit the chaplain to receive his blessing before each mission. Once he asked the chaplain, 'Don't you think the German military men are visiting their chaplains, too?' So you ask, 'Whose side is God on?' We know He was with us during the war. But at the time you may wonder what God wants us to do. Thus, your faith must be the strongest part of your life—faith and a guardian angel."

John C. Playter
Ex-POW, WWII, Bataan Death March

"At a very early age, I learned from my father to be honest and trustworthy. Dad was only seen at church during weddings or funerals, but his example depicted Christian principles. Mom was the 'churchgoer' and I went with her. The importance of Bible study was prominent in her life and this led to my profession of faith at the age of 14. Although not being as good and as fervent a student of the Bible as I should have been, I learned, and have never forgotten, the Lord's prayer and recognized and have always tried to practice what is said in Matthew 6:33.

"Being overseas when World War II began, I soon realized that

I was serving a nation that was not prepared for war and I was serving with troops sorely disappointed with our nation. Lack of materiel and lack of food and medicine soon took its toll. After only four months of no Allied assistance, we became prisoners of ruthless captors who placed little value on human life.

"Forced to work with little food and medicine, I survived two years and five months. Daily prayers for strength and hope were raised. But the daily indignities by our captors and even a forced affront to my loyalty to America, tended to make prayer seem futile. A forced loading onto a 'hellship' brought a change. Seventeen days, yet traveling only a very short distance, brought direct hits by two American-fired torpedoes. This freed 82 of us but brought death to 668.

"At the request of a fellow prisoner, I traded locations with him less than two minutes before the torpedoes struck—I survived, he didn't. For 54 years I wondered why I survived but other God-fearing men didn't. The only explanation has to be answered prayer. Fear of, but trusting God, is required of us all."

Captain J. Charles Plumb
U.S. Navy (Ret.)
Ex-POW Vietnam

"When asked to offer advice about success, I am reminded of the advice my high school football coach, Clancy Smith, a wounded WWI veteran, gave me. After the final game of a one-in-seven losing season, I said, 'I'm sorry, coach, I guess we're just a bunch of losers.' I still remember his words, 'Son, whether you think this team is a bunch of losers or a bunch of winners, you're right.'

"The next day I asked Coach Smith, 'I don't understand, what do you mean?' 'Whether you think you're a loser or a winner, you're right.' He explained, 'The difference between success and failure is you, and it's a choice.'

"I am an ex-Navy fighter pilot with 75 combat missions over Vietnam. If I had it all to do over again, I would stop at 74. The Vietnamese cell I was in was eight feet long and eight feet wide. I could pace three steps one way, then turn around and pace three steps the other. Inside this cell, there were no books to read, no window to look out, no TV, telephone, or radio. I didn't have a pencil or a piece of paper for 2,103 days.

"I spent six years at the 'University of Hanoi,' and I received a degree in 'hard knocks.' It was a long time to pace three steps in one direction and then three steps in the other. I would not wish it on anyone. I would, however, tell you it was the most valuable six years of my life.

"For two of the almost six years I was a POW in Vietnam, I served as the chaplain to the POWs. I feel I must stress the importance of faith as a key to significance. Finally, if there is one single thing I validated in that Communist prison camp, it's this: Coach Smith was right! The difference between failure, success, and also significance, is you, and it's your choice!"

Chief Warrant Officer Charles L. Pruitt, U.S. Navy (Ret.)
Ex-POW, Bataan, Corregidor, Philippines, Japan

"I was a veteran of the Philippine campaign in the early days of WWII, having served on both the Bataan Peninsula and the Island fortress of Corregidor. I spent 41 months as a prisoner of war of the Japanese, surviving the slave labor camps in the Philippines and Japan, and the 'hell ships' transporting the POWs to Japan and other foreign lands.

"I would credit my survival to my faith in God, country, self, and my comrades. We helped one another when help was needed, without becoming dependent on each other. When help was needed in the form of moral support, it was always there without the asking. My creed was not to become dependent on others but to know when to ask for help and to accept it when necessary."

Dudley Riley
Ex-POW, WWII, Germany

"As a young boy growing up in rural Kentucky, and the youngest of nine children, the value of the family unit was strongly emphasized. Because of my strong family foundations and my Christian upbringing, the desire to live and to be of service to others was firmly established for me prior to my years spent as a Prisoner of War in World War II.

"Today I am grateful that I have been given the opportunities to serve and to help others through my involvement with the Red Cross Disaster Relief, teaching Sunday School to the elderly that are homebound, lecturing elementary and high school students about my experiences as a prisoner of war, and working with exchange students to help with the English language and history of the United States.

"I retired from the Veterans Administration after 35 years. I was elected to serve as State Commander of the Kentucky Department of Ex-POWs in 1996-1997, and again in 1998-1999. I have been commander of the local western Kentucky Chapter since its formation in February 1995. I am proud to work with my fellow Ex-POW friends to make life better for all Americans. After all, 'We exist to help those who cannot help themselves.'

"My code of conduct for life has been to establish a firm foundation in God and family and serve them in the ways in which I have been called upon to do so. This brings to mind the words of the grand old hymn:

I sing because I'm happy; I sing because I'm FREE

His eye is on the sparrow, And I know He watches me."

Norman Rippee
Ex-POW, WWII, Germany

"I was inducted into the Army Air Corps in 1942. I volunteered for gunnery school, becoming a flight engineer on a combat crew of a B-26 Bomber of the 319th Bombardment Group. After graduation, we were sent to North Africa. We had ten crews in our class, two of which crashed with no survivors. This was perhaps the first of many points in my life where I knew our lives were in the hand of God.

"From north Africa, we went to Sardinia and then Corsica. On October 19th, 1944, I was on my 22nd mission in the Po Valley of Italy when I was shot down by Luftwaffe ME109 fighter planes. We all parachuted out and immediately became prisoners of war. Again, I knew His hand would protect me.

"I was picked up by soldiers of the Afrika Korps and sent to northwest Poland, to the prison camp of Stalag Luft IV. On February 6, 1945, the Luftwaffe marched us out of Luft IV because the Russian army would soon overrun the camp. We marched west, sleeping in barns and sometimes outside on the ground, for 86 days. During this period, we never removed our clothing or our shoes. Food and water were scarce. I lost a great deal of weight.

"On May 2, 1945, the English 2nd Army caught up with us

approximately 100K east of Hamburg, Germany. We had covered approximately 600 miles on this forced march. We arrived at the Canadian base in Brussels on May 8, 1945. I never once doubted that I would return home.

"I feel fortunate to be a citizen of this country. Even though I came out of WWII with some physical and mental scars, they have healed long ago. If called upon to do it again, I would gladly go. God bless America."

Brigadier General Robinson Risner
U.S. Air Force (Ret.)
Ex-POW, Vietnam

"Few persons have reached their goal without determination. During my 33 year Air Force career, I was surrounded by people who were better educated, had a higher IQ, and greater talent. However, few had more determination. In addition, I had a strong faith in God. Determination and faith in God are the lynch pins that will take you to your goal."

Zach Roberts
Ex-POW, WWII, Germany
National Commander, AX-POWs 1999-2000

"It is my conviction that the most significant legacy we can provide our children and grandchildren is a strong sense of religious and moral values.

"My maternal grandmother taught herself to read and write, and taught adult Bible classes; from her, I learned faith, honesty, and integrity. My maternal grandfather was a coal miner who suffered multiple severe injuries; from him, I learned strength in adversity. At the height of the depression years, my mother opened a successful business; from her, I learned the value of hard work. From my father, I learned to have kindness and compassion for the less fortunate and to have a positive attitude.

"I make slide presentations to every new class at the NCO Academy at McGuire Air Force Base, and their most commonly asked question is how I endured 15 months of captivity and post-traumatic stress. My response is that in every person's life they will face a time of crisis with no one to turn to. Alcohol and drugs cannot solve our problems. I am not a preacher, but I am a believer. I credit faith—the belief that it is the grace of God that gives us the support and guidance to persevere. I am alive today because of Him. It has been the legacy of this faith that told me God watched over me, and Jesus walked with me.

"My faith was tested today. As I was writing this advice, I was informed my son, Master Sergeant Zach Sheldon Roberts, age 47, had died of a massive heart attack. I am comforted knowing that God will watch over him, and Jesus will walk with him."

Ralph Rodriguez, Jr.
Ex-POW, WWII, Bataan
National Commander, AX-POWs 1964–65

"More than a half century ago, I was drafted into the service of my country. In those days, the thought was: 'Why worry about the war in Europe? We are safely guarded by two great oceans of water.'

"As a young man, I had never been away from home. I was more prepared than I realized. I knew that my tour of duty was for one year, and I was proud of being a soldier. As soldiers we didn't just walk to town, we marched in cadence. Within a few months, we overcame the recruit status; we were real soldiers. Suddenly everything I was taught at home by my parents started to come into play.

"Being one of ten brothers and sisters, I knew how to obey authority. Being true and honest to my superiors was not my first test. I was educated in Catholic school, by nuns, and grew up in a community that practiced faith, honesty, integrity, and good moral values. These qualities were embedded in our minds.

"After about six months in the army, our regiment was on its way to the Philippines. The possibility of war expressed by our leaders maintained that we were a great and powerful nation and if Japan dare attack us, we would destroy the enemy within six months. How wrong we were!

"On December 8th, 1941, at 7 A.M., just as we stepped out of church, we heard that the Japanese had bombed Pearl Harbor and that the damage was enormous and the loss of life was great.

At 12:25 p.m., just after lunch, the beginning of what was to be a six month war began. Thirty minutes after the Japanese bombers dropped their bombs on Clark Field, in the Philippines, I was headed for the hospital. I was a medic, but a soldier called me to help him feed ammunition to his 50 caliber machine gun. We emptied four boxes of ammunition at the dive bombers. The planes strafed us, but we kept firing. About 5 P.M., I was on my way to Nichols Field in the city of Manila. The enemy continued to bomb us constantly.

"By the end of December, we were sent to the Bataan peninsula. Our resistance began to crumble against a powerful enemy with a great number of troops. This was the beginning of the end of the predicted six month war. There was complete cooperation in an attempt to survive. We all helped each other. As our numbers decreased, we gained strength and determination against the enemy. I searched my soul to find answers about our future.

"Our Catholic priest would come once a week to hold chapel services. I asked the chaplain his honest opinion of what was in store for us. His answer was a shock to my ears when he said, 'SURRENDER!' It's difficult to explain the preparation for surrender. The commander of the medical company, holding a white flag, walked down the hill toward the road where enemy tanks were waiting. We faced the enemy, their machine guns pointed directly at us. Our six month war came to an end in four brutal months. We were suffering from disease and hunger. We were out of ammunition, food, and medical supplies.

"Once again the character I had developed from my childhood and as a young man suddenly began to spring into action—love thy neighbor, feed the hungry, care for the sick. As a medic, that was my duty until the last day of imprisonment.

"On January 30th, 1945, at 7:30 P.M., the 6th Ranger Battalion rescued about 511 weak, sick men. Once again we marched, although this time we marched the freedom march. We marched all night and by noon the next day we reached the American lines.

"My advice to both the young and the old is: When you help those in need, you're doing God's work. When you're dedicated to God's work, you will overcome any and all difficulties. Thank God, I am a survivor."

John Romine
Ex-POW, WWII, Germany
National Chaplain, AX-POWs

"As a child during the depression days in Oklahoma, so many things seemed huge and awesome and far too great for my understanding—the great prayers and sermons at church, the sheriff, and leaders of our community. Then I was caught up in a 'World War.'

"I flew 43 combat missions of the most hellish kind in a B-24 bomber. I was shot down over Northern Italy and became a POW in Germany for 11 months of hunger, thirst, sickness, fear, cold, and filth.

"After liberation and returning home, I was in total shock and refused to participate in worship, church services, or honoring a God who would allow people to go through what happened to me.

"Then one day I read Matthew 25. I remembered what a few swallows of water had meant to me, handed to me from a window as we passed through a small village, by a total stranger one dark night while on a forced march from one POW camp to another.

"I had found the answer and went to work for the Lord. Lend a helping hand when and where you can. Even small deeds are eternal."

Chief Warrant Officer 4
Wilburn Rowden
U.S. Army National Guard
(Ret.)
Ex-POW, Germany

"*Courage*—To accomplish your assigned goals even under the most adverse conditions. You need courage to press on toward the achievement of a goal. I have observed during my confinement and harassment and the harsh conditions as a POW this evidence of courage. When the future looked bleak, those men with courage made the best of the situation. This also included careful planning to eliminate or circumvent the obstacles that could hinder or prevent accomplishment of your assigned or personal goals.

"*Faith*—Plays a great part in accomplishing your goals. My observation is, faith is greatest under the most adverse conditions. As a POW, I observed young men as well as myself eager to learn more of the Bible and its teachings. Of the few classes that were permitted, those about the Bible were attended by more young soldiers. We were permitted to have church services on occasion and the attendance attested to a faith and a belief in God.

"*Consideration*—For people you are working with and especially the people you are training or leading. A sense of caring for their safety and well-being will make them respectful of you as their teacher and leader. Work to gain the respect of people you associate and/or work with.

"*Love of Country*—The POW was always expressing and displaying a love of country and they were always looking forward to the day they would return to our country and our way of life. Always strive to be the best you can be."

Rear Admiral Robert Shumaker
U.S. Navy, (Ret.)
Ex-POW, Vietnam

"Paradoxically, I learned a lot about life from my experience as a prisoner of war in Vietnam. Those tough lessons learned within a jail cell have application to all those who will never have to undergo that particular trauma. At some point in life everybody will be hungry, cold, lonely, extorted, sick, humiliated, or fearful in varying degrees of intensity. It is the manner in which you react to these challenges that will distinguish you.

"When adversity strikes, you've got to fall back with the punch and do your best to get up off the mat to come back for the next round. Realize that a person is not in total control of his destiny, but you need to know what your goals are, and you have to prepare yourself in advance to take advantage of opportunity when that door opens. Some important tools on the road to success include the ability and willingness to communicate, treating those around you with respect and courtesy no matter what their station in life might be, and conducting your life with the morality and behavior that will allow you to face yourself…for in the end, you alone must be your own harshest critic."

Major Ira Simpson
U.S. Air Force (Ret.)
Ex-POW, WWII, Germany

"As a young boy growing up during the depression years, I was taught by my parents, church leaders, and teachers to have faith in God, my country, and my fellow man.

"My faith in God and in answered prayer served me well during the days of my imprisonment in a German prisoner of war camp. I knew that with God's help I would survive the starvation, cruel treatment, and denial of my freedom. I also knew that many people were praying for me, and that God answers prayer.

"Because of my faith in my country, I was certain that I was not forgotten and that the prisoners would be liberated by our armed forces as soon as they could reach us. I had no doubts that we would be free again.

"The willingness of the men in the camp to help others by sharing small amounts of food that were received, assisting those who were ill, and providing companionship sustained my faith in my fellow man. There were many examples of compassion, kindness to others, and friendship too numerous to mention. I know of no other group of men who were so dedicated to those around them.

"I have continued to live by this faith during my military and civilian career, and I find my faith to be important to my relationship with others and the basis of any success I have achieved. I believe that these principles are ones that will make any life successful and significant."

Ralph Sirianni
Ex-POW, WWII, Germany

"I live by these three words: pride, respect, and attitude. I feel children should be taught at an early age the significance of these three words. If they live by them, they would become good people and good Americans. I also live by the Ten Commandments, and respect every person's religious beliefs and practices, whatever they may be.

"I have had the honor, privilege, and opportunity to serve my town as an elected member of the Board of Health, and a town meeting member. On the state level, I was elected to the Massachusetts Legislature for ten years. For almost 60 years, I served my country. I served in the United States Army Air Corps, as a staff sergeant, and as a right waist gunner on a B-17 flying fortress. I have been richly blessed in my 66 years of service, living by pride, respect, and attitude, and always attempting to live by the Ten Commandments."

Jack Sites
Ex-POW, WWII, Bulgaria

"I was a ball turret gunner on a B-24 bomber during World War II. On July 26th, 1944, while on my 16th mission over Albania, my airplane and crew were shot down by enemy fire. We were captured and held prisoner for more than 10 months. Those 10 months were the longest 10 months of my life. This experience in survival is one that I will never forget. I remember watching my fellow crew members being subjected to terrible beatings while in a Bulgarian prison camp.

"One of our crew members was a Jewish officer. During our torture, the members of our crew were asked to sign a document that stated that this crew member (the Jewish officer) had ordered us to kill German women and children. Although we suffered numerous beatings, not one of the crew would sign this document. The horrible conditions and treatment that followed are too painful to discuss. Many of my friends and other servicemen died while held prisoner.

"I learned as a prisoner of war to have faith in my God, my family, my country, and my comrades. Even after such a terrible ordeal and seeing how awful one man can be toward another, I still believe that there is something good in everyone. I strive every day to find that good thing in everyone I encounter. The good in people is there; you might have to look deeper in some than in others, but I assure you, it is still there. You must have faith in God and faith in each other. Righteousness will prevail."

Edward Slater
Ex-POW, Korea

"I was in the 21st infantry regiment of the 24th Division when the Korean War started. We were sent into combat at Osan, Korea on July 5, 1950, to stem the tide of the advancing North Koreans. My unit was overrun by a horde of North Koreans. I escaped capture for two weeks by hiding in caves, bushes, and ditches in the mountains. Finally, worn out, very hungry and thirsty, I was captured in a village where I had been befriended by an old couple who fed me and gave me water. However, it was possible that they may have called the North Korean soldiers who captured me.

"From that point on, my life in Korea was a living hell! I was beaten routinely. I was denied food and water for long periods of time. I was paraded in front of the civilian population for propaganda purposes. I was interrogated, tortured, and suffered through the heat and cold for the next few months. I was almost convinced that God had forgotten me.

"After many, long hard miles of marching northward on my bleeding, bare feet, we were finally put aboard a train. Unfortunately, the train was shot up by our fighter bombers. As a result, the guards went into a frenzy and started machine gunning the prisoners. I fell under the pile. I was wounded, but not badly. The guards poured diesel fuel over us and left us for dead. A friend, Bob, was lying on top of me badly wounded and bleeding on me. (Bob survived because I later brought help to him.) I finally worked my way free and went back down the tracks to the train station where I promptly fell asleep! When I awoke, there was a young boy there who, in pretty good English, said, 'Follow me and I will get you food.' He said he had learned English from some G.I.s. He took me to a nearby hut where an old lady fed me. While eating, I heard a commotion outside the door. The door suddenly slid open and there stood an Angel!!

"This angel was a 6' 2" Master Sergeant. He took my hand and said, 'Let me take you home.' So you see, not all angels come equipped with a halo and wings! Some come in the form of Master Sergeants!

"God had not forgotten me after all!"

Lieutenant Colonel John S. Smith, U.S. Air Force (Ret.)
Ex-POW, WWII, Russia

"Personality, self confidence, honesty, and morality—The right mixture of these traits will ensure a successful life and career. Treating people with respect and dignity plus developing a work philosophy that will entice people to willingly work for you and with you is a must. You cannot succeed individually—all great leaders are partially judged on their advisors.

"Self confidence is self-explanatory. Believe in and trust yourself above all others. Be willing to trust your own judgement in making decisions.

"Honesty and morality go hand in hand. These traits are developed during childhood and should be expanded during your lifetime as experience dictates."

William W. Smith
Ex-POW, Korea

"I was a young career soldier caught up in combat in North Korea, where I was held captive by the North Korean and Chinese Communists for 2 1/2 years. I survived by the will of God and the prayers of my grandmother. My total faith, mixed with pure 'cussedness,' gave me the will not to give up.

"The long days and the dark nights were spent helping the sick and wounded and gave little time to think about self. My greatest pain was seeing my buddies die. You wonder, why them and not me? Then you realize that it is in God's will, and He is not yet ready for you.

"All who came out of the ordeal came out with integrity, honor, and pride in having done our duty even when it wasn't easy.

"My code of conduct has always been to try to do what I believe is right and everything will fall into place. Remember: 'All things work together for good to those who love the Lord.'"

Clifford L. Stumpf
Ex-POW, WWII, Germany

"My service with the armed forces took me to both the Pacific and the European theaters of war. I firmly believe my faith in God and a strong will to live brought me through a terrible ordeal. I was in the 106th Division that was virtually wiped out in the Battle of the Bulge. After a three-day battle in an encirclement, I was captured on December 19, 1944, one of the coldest winters on record. I did not remove my clothes for six months.

"As a POW I was still in the Army, but under an entirely different command. There were no good assignments; however, some of the areas of confinement were better than others. My belief is that if the good Lord allowed you to come home, then that was the best assignment for you.

"We were transferred often by rail in boxcars. Cold and hunger were always with us. After our arrival at one location, we were sent out on different details: some were sent to farm labor, some to mines, others to factories, and any place labor was needed. I was one of 100 men sent to the city of Dresden, Germany. Dresden was declared an open city and appeared to be a safe place. That all changed when the German Army began to move war material into the city.

"I had to work on trolley freight cars, delivering freight throughout the city. One day after a bombing, our tracks were damaged and had to be repaired before we could return to our camp. Nearby a German home was damaged. While we were waiting for the repair, five of us were allowed to help the family straighten up their home. When we were ready to leave, this family risked their lives by leaving each of us a sandwich by a stack of boards. We were so starved. The memory of that sandwich has remained with me all of my life.

"A few days later, bombings left Dresden almost completely destroyed. I have often wondered if that family survived. I have questioned what I would have done if I had been in that family's situation. This experience instilled in me a lesson taught in the Bible: Do good, if you can, to the person you believe might be your enemy. In this instance, an enemy gave a cold and hungry American soldier a sandwich which I believe helped to revive my faith and hope to live and to be able to return home to the United States of America."

Wright S. Swanay
Ex-POW, WWII, Germany

"I believe that my experience as a prisoner of war in Germany during World War II instilled in me a sense of duty that has motivated me all my life. It inspired me to live a life of loyalty and service—to my family, to my comrades, to my country, and to my God.

"I am the last of my family. Fondly I recall the family ties and the sacrifices that helped us through the depression, through World War II, and the years that followed. It fell on me to bury them all and settle their affairs. I have few regrets, a million rich and happy memories, and a duty to represent them well to the generations that will follow us.

"For many years now I have served as a Veterans Service Officer at the local, state, and national level, helping my comrades gain benefits to which they were entitled. This has brought me great satisfaction and great reward.

"I served my country when called upon in WWII. Unlike Nathan Hale of Revolutionary War fame, I spoke no great words as a POW, just the required name, rank, and serial number.

"In serving others I feel I have served my Creator. My creed is found in the book of Micah in the Old Testament, chapter 6, verse 8, '...What doth the Lord require of thee, but to do justly, and to love mercy and to walk humbly with thy God.'"

Captain Charles Nels Tanner U.S. Navy (Ret.)
Ex-POW Vietnam

"Several truths of life were driven home to me during my 6 years as a POW in North Vietnam. No man is perfect. Perfect or not, he must continue to do his very best. Without God's help, real victory for a man is impossible. To get God's help, you must ask for it. In turn, you must provide help to your fellow man. The love of your fellow man is vital to life. Men cannot lead successfully without proving they are willing to follow.

"Although I received most of these truths as a child, they had been put aside and taken for granted until the test of my life was staring me in the face. All this took only a split second, after many years of trust in my personal skills and faith in the technology of man. All this has nothing to do with the Vietnam War. It could have happened anywhere, anytime. Do not wait for the revelation. It could easily be too late!"

Merle G. "Gil" Turley
Ex-POW, WWII, Germany

"The motto of the American ex-POW is 'freedom is not free.' This one small statement is the most forgotten, ignored, unappreciated grouping of words by the people of the United States today. Think of Memorial Day, how many people remember why we really have this day on our calendar? Then, there is Veteran's Day. Who attends the parades? National Ex-POW's Day—who thanks a veteran or ex-POW for their sacrifice so everyone can enjoy the freedom they have in this country? A common saying of the ex-POW is 'freedom, ask us.' This is truly a question we can answer. Not only were we combat veterans, but we have gone one step further. Our freedom was taken from us, we were humiliated, starved, beaten, lost our self-esteem, experienced loneliness, and lost all the benefits of freedom. All we had to fight this experience was our faith. We had faith that our country would liberate us. We had faith that our families would remember and pray for us. Last, but not least, we had faith in a Supreme Being and that He was looking after us and would liberate us from this trial. All of us ex-POWs kept this bottled up within ourselves after we were liberated until the past few years because we felt that no one would believe our experiences. We did not seek others' sympathy. We only wanted to be recognized as the defenders of their freedom, the freedom they enjoy today.

"All of us must have faith in country, family, friends, God, and ourselves."

Chief Master Sergeant Maynard "Doc" Unger
U.S. Air Force (Ret.)
Ex-POW, WWII, Germany

"The Lord spared my life and I am constantly reminding myself that He must have something in mind for me. I truly believe He has directed my life. I certainly didn't plan it. It just happened. My faith in God brought me through WWII, including 22 months in a German prisoner of war experience. Did it change me? Certainly, and for the best! I now have a high level of patriotism, God-given talent, and a desire to serve others. My faith, confidence, reliability, and reasonably good health have allowed me to be placed in positions of leadership ever since my POW experience. In all these opportunities, I have striven to do my best. I hope to be remembered for service to God, my family, and to others."

Emilio "Vince" Vizachero, Jr.
Ex-POW, WWII, Germany

"My code of conduct as an American POW in WWII was as follows: To our captors we gave only our name, rank and serial number. When our captors ordered us to do forced labor at gunpoint, we did so. When our captors ordered us to make propaganda statements while subjected to torture, we steadfastly refused. When our captors offered us extra food and water if we would denounce our country, we told them we would rather die first.

"We, American ex-prisoners of war, were the spirit of America. Our absolute dedication to God gave us hope and courage to endure the pain and suffering. When Jesus Christ my Savior was at the door, I didn't hesitate to open the door. The long and painful months as a German POW changed my life forever, but God gave me the courage to endure the suffering.

"I wrote the following poem as a POW in Augsburg, Germany.

"Looking through the barbed wire fence
 at those wild daisies, oh how I envy such freedom!

Trying to reach through the fence
to pick a handful,
 but they evaded my clutching hand.

It had to be God's way,
 giving me hope and faith to survive.
So when droplets of tears come to your eyes,
 just clutch a handful of God's wild daisies."

Glenn A. Wade
Ex-POW, WWII, Germany

"I was a navigator in World War II. I grew up in the depth of the depression, and being a Christian certainly gave me strength to take whatever the Germans handed me. I was a POW in Germany for over 27 months. Padre McDonald always preached that God was not responsible for the predicament we were in, and that God and Jesus would see us through.

"We needed courage and faith to be an honorable servant to the USA. Attitude and how we spent our time was very important in surviving such a difficult ordeal. We always tried to believe we would make it through; we had good training; and we were disciplined to do whatever we needed to do. We spent our time improving our minds and keeping physically strong, having classes, reading, arts, and competitive sports."

Robert Waldrop
Ex-POW, WWII, Germany, Stalag IV and VI

"I would give the following advice to those in the military:

"Stay in the best physical condition possible to be better prepared for any difficult assignments or hardships that you may encounter.

"In the same manner, absorb the best training that is offered.

"Continually practice self-discipline.

"Communicate well with others as to offer hope for survival and set the example of a 'never-give-up attitude.'

"All of the above will be much easier to accomplish if you maintain your faith in God, your country, and your loved ones. All of the above should be adhered to in everyday life whether you are in the military or any walk of life."

Edgar D. Whitcomb
Ex-POW, Corregidor
Former Governor, Indiana

"Success is earned, not necessarily crafted. It is attainable by all persons of all means and backgrounds. The hallmark for success is quite basic: to be in service to the Lord and to use the gifts He has entrusted to each of us for that purpose. How this is accomplished though is of utmost importance. The values of honesty, integrity, work ethic, and the compassion of 'Do unto others...' mark the way we approach and accomplish life's work. How well we combine these determines personal success. How well this is accomplished in the eyes of the Lord determines significance."

PART IV
POLITICAL LEADERS

PRESIDENT

The President of the United States is often considered the most powerful elected official in the world. Forty-two men have served as President. The constitution establishes only three qualifications for a President: He/she must be at least 35 years old, have lived in the United States at least 14 years, and be a natural born citizen. The Presidential candidate is nominated by a political party convention and is elected by a majority vote of the Electoral College. The President is elected for a four-year term and may not be elected more than twice.

CONGRESS

Congress is a bicameral (two-chambered) legislature. The 100-member Senate consists of two Senators from each of the 50 states. The House of Representatives, usually called the House, has 435 members. House members, or representatives, are elected from congressional districts. Every state must have at least one House seat. Representatives are often called Congressmen or Congresswomen, though the titles also apply to Senators. The qualifications for the Senate are: He/she must be at least 30 years old, a U.S. citizen for at least 9 years, and a resident of the state from which the candidate seeks election. The qualifications for the House are: He/she must be at least 25 years old, a U.S. citizen for at least 7 years, and a resident of the state from which the candidate seeks election. Nominations: Nearly all candidates for the Congress are nominated in primary elections. Elections: A Senator is elected by the voters from all parts of the state. A Representative may be elected by the voters of one congressional district or be elected at large by voters throughout the state. Terms: Senators are elected to six-year terms and Representatives are elected to two-year terms.

GOVERNOR

The Governor is the chief executive of a state. Governors serve for four years in most states, and for two years in a few states. Their duties, like those of the President of the United States, are partly executive, partly legislative, and partly judicial.

"Everyone must submit himself to the governing authorities, for there is no authority except that which God has established....

Do you want to be free from fear of the one in authority? Then do what is right and he will commend you. For he is God's servant to do you good"
(Romans 13:1,3-4).

Wayne Allard R
Senator, Colorado

"Respect your mother and father, and have faith in God. Don't be afraid to set goals and experiment. If your first goal doesn't work out, you should always have secondary goals. We all experience failure sometimes in our lives, but you pick yourself up and try again. That is what living is all about; that is what this country is all about.

"I never went to veterinary school to become a U.S. Senator. The opportunity arose due to circumstances I could have never expected. My belief in God and my family gave me the courage to take on new challenges. Never be afraid to take on new and exciting challenges."

John Ashcroft R
Former Senator, Missouri
U.S. Attorney General

"I want to share the pledge that every member of my office has taken. It is a pledge of service, commitment, and dedication. It is a pledge we want to share with the American people. I am grateful for the blessings I have received through the prayers of many people from around the country. In my service to the state of Missouri over the years, my faith in God and reliance upon His grace has been constant. My faith provides the foundation of all I do in my personal and political life. I invited the presence of God into my life as a young person and I continue to do that daily."

David M. Beasley
Former Governor, South Carolina

"There is no greater honor than to be called a man of virtue. Virtue implies moral excellence. To be excellent in anything requires diligence. I strive to diligently serve my Lord, my family, and my state—in that order. It is through God's grace that I am in a position to have any positive effect on the State of South Carolina. He has put me in a role of leadership, and I am here to further His cause by promoting messages that focus on family, individual responsibility, and responsible government. Putting His will above my own desires is the course I seek each day."

Christopher S. Bond
Senator, Missouri

"There are many standards to which one can hold during life's travels. One of the best philosophies I have heard is contained in a statement by my friend, Congressman J.C. Watts from Oklahoma. He says, 'Character is measured by what we do when no one is watching.' If you are of strong character and hold yourself to this belief, every decision you have to make will be clear."

Bill Bradley
Former Senator, New Jersey

"Success in life is not about personal accomplishments or wealth. Sometimes the smallest things with meaning are more important than the biggest things without meaning. What matters is leading a life that helps others. Whether in a position of visibility or anonymity, all of us can make a difference in improving the circumstances of others.

"In addition, it is important to work hard and be prepared for life's challenges. As Ed Macauley, former NBA basketball player and my high school basketball camp director said, 'When you're not practicing, remember someone somewhere is practicing; and when you meet, given roughly equal ability, he'll win.' I never wanted to lose because I wasn't prepared, whether in basketball or politics."

Terry E. Branstad
Former Governor, Iowa

"The people of Iowa have given me the great honor and privilege of serving a record 16 years as Governor. My direct and straightforward approach to public service has always been one of total honesty. I have tried my best to rely upon a sense of fairness that treats friend and foe alike with respect and dignity.

"Enthusiasm, hard work, and an openness to debate and discuss issues have helped me to be responsive to the people. Public service is all about giving of yourself to help others.

"A leader must articulate a vision and develop a strategic plan to achieve that vision. The plan should be adjusted and perfected over time as new information and knowledge is obtained. An incremental approach to continuous improvement can achieve much over time. It is critically important never to lose sight of the goals that you set for yourself and for your organization.

"As governor in the mid-1980s, I had the challenging task of leading Iowa through the difficult period of the Farm Crisis. I will be forever grateful that Rev. Robert H. Schuller was kind enough to send me a copy of his book, *Tough Times Never Last, but Tough People Do!* I have often referred to the wisdom that the book offered. The title alone provides motivation to continue to work toward your goals, even in the face of adversity.

"An honest, clean, efficient, responsive, and fiscally prudent state government is my goal. A hands-on, enthusiastic approach that demonstrates a passion for achieving the desired goals is part of my personal creed. If something is worth doing, it should be done well, with vigor, passion, and enthusiasm."

Conrad Burns
Senator, Montana

"I maintain that success is what one defines for him or herself. Public service is a high calling, and a high degree of dedication and integrity are required. Forty hours a week doesn't get it. Working just for money doesn't get it. Dedication to a higher ideal and a vision for the next generation does."

George Bush
Former U.S. President

"My Navy service affected my later life in public service. I learned a lot about human nature. I saw men under great stress. I saw men die in front of my eyes. I lost friends. I saw a war in which the military were given whatever they needed to get the job done. I learned a lot about heroism and honor and love of country. I learned about teamwork. I learned about loyalty.

"On September 2, 1944, 53 years ago, I was shot down in combat over a Japanese-held island. I was a scared young man who had just turned 20 years old. Two crewmen were killed. I survived, a submarine out on War Patrol, having picked me up. I have wondered often why me—why was I spared when others died? I'll never know the answer to this question. I do know that terrifying experience helped me become a man. It strengthened my faith. It made me count my blessings for a loving family and for friends."

George W. Bush
Former Governor, Texas
President of the United States

"I have been alive now for more than half a century. The last 50 years have seen the most profound cultural change in American history. The role of government has grown dramatically, while the role of the individual has declined. By trying to do too much, government has undermined one of America's greatest strengths: individual potential. Because we are free individuals, our capacity to dream and to do is as vast as the west Texas sky. Throughout the ages, individuals, more than armies or nations or politics, have shaped the course of events. Every triumphant achievement, every great decision, every spark of genius, every act of compassion in the final analysis came about because of the acts of individuals. Each of us holds a piece of the promise of America—each one of us, not just a few—not just those of certain income or neighborhood or skin color or educational level, every single one of us."

Arne H. Carlson
Former Governor, Minnesota

"I believe people are successful when they are true to their convictions, contributing members of their community, and lifetime learners. Being true to your convictions is not always easy, and you may be lonely in some of your decisions. Rest assured though, that the loneliness will dissipate over time and arm you with the knowledge you need to succeed in whatever task you take on. Finally, always remember your community. As you take from your community, so too must you give back to your community."

Lawton Chiles
Former Governor, Florida

"My years of service to our nation's government have given me an opportunity to learn many things. One of the first things I learned was to listen to people. They really care about their communities and our nation. I learned that the way to achieve leadership is to learn more about your subject than anyone else.

"Work hard instead of looking for shortcuts. Leadership isn't about winning, it's about fighting the right fights. Leadership requires that you fight for the things you believe in. Dare to be bold. Reach beyond your grasp to go beyond the path that you can see. Most importantly, listen to your inner voice and do what your heart tells you is right. Public service is a challenging and rewarding vocation. I am proud to have served the people of this great nation and this wonderful state."

Thomas Carper
Former Governor
Senator, Delaware

"Among the keys to leading a life that is both successful and significant are these four:

1. Do what is right.
2. Do your best in all that you do.
3. Treat others as you would have them treat you.
4. Never give up.

"The secret to knowing real happiness throughout our lives is even simpler—serve others. People look for happiness in all kinds of places: money, power, fame, material possessions, drugs, alcohol ,to mention a few. Those things may provide a sense of happiness for a period of time, but one source of enduring happiness that will never let us down is to find someone in our lives who needs help and then to help them. It isn't hard to find them either. They are all around us."

John Engler
Governor, Michigan

"On the day of my first inauguration, a friend and mentor, former Michigan Governor George Romney, gave me two words of powerful leadership advice.

"It takes boldness to reach your potential—to set sail on your own course and hold to it against the winds of doubt and defeat. To be bold is to attempt what some say cannot be done, to make decisions that are difficult and unpopular, and to accept responsibility for the outcome, whether you succeed or fail.

"The strength and wisdom to be bold comes from a trusting faith in God. Through His grace and goodness, the ordinary can become extraordinary and the impossible made possible."

Lauch Faircloth
Former Senator, North Carolina

"The fundamental characteristic that is common to all successful people—a necessary characteristic without which, in fact, success is virtually impossible—is an unlimited belief in themselves. To achieve any goal, it is first necessary to be able to imagine oneself having already achieved it. Nothing has stopped more people in their tracks than an inability to believe they 'can.'

"While an unbounded belief in one's own ability is necessary, it is by no means sufficient. The other inescapable fact of life is the need to work hard. There is no shortcut. Nothing of value was ever achieved by cutting corners. Vision without follow-through is mere daydreaming."

Wendell H. Ford
Senator, Kentucky

"Two different quotations immediately come to mind. The first is from James 2:17, 'Faith without works is dead.' For me, this quotation is a reminder that our work takes on meaning through deep faith, and our faith takes on life with hard work. I think that's an important lesson no matter what kind of work you do, but it's especially important when crafting policy that will affect so many people's day-to-day lives. It's a reminder that faith and hard work must go hand-in-hand. No matter how strongly you believe in something, you can't accomplish your goals without hard work. Nor will hard work amount to much if you don't have a deep-seated belief in what you are pursuing.

"The second quote is from Kentuckian Henry Clay's famous speech in 1850 before the U.S. Senate on preserving the Union, where he described compromise as 'mutual sacrifice.' For me, that quote speaks to an important balance Clay struck between his staunch independence and his belief in joining into the social contract through public service. The life of Henry Clay teaches Americans that we can hold fast to the spirit of independence on which this nation was founded without undermining the ethic of public service which holds this nation together. If we see public service as a call to higher ourselves, we can make a difference while remaining true to ourselves. The power of those words literally held the nation together as it confronted some of its most difficult questions. I have found them to be a powerful tool over the years as I work with other legislators to hammer out differences."

M.J. "Mike" Foster, Jr.
Governor, Louisiana

"The following best describes my idea of moving from success to significance: When I review those projects that I have considered successes, I find that each success was made possible by a clear vision of how the future might be different and better, motivation to make the necessary changes, and a willingness to take the risks to make the difference. The attributes I learned in scouting are still valid: a dedication to the task at hand and pride in what you do. Just do your best, but be selective in what you do. Tithe your time, and cultivate and rely upon a deep faith in your God with compassion and respect for other people and their differences. Enjoy life."

Jim Geringer
Governor, Wyoming

"The advice I would like to offer is to take time for public service. Our country will not survive in freedom if our people don't take part in our processes of freedom. I urge you to spend some time in public service. Start with your family and friends. Give them your support. The basic unit of government is your family. And the most elemental unit of democracy is your community. Be a volunteer in your church and in your community. You may even see a time when you are asked to run for public office. Consider that to be a noble calling. But be guided by civic responsibility, not by desire for attention."

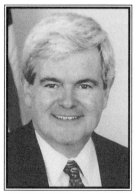

Newt Gingrich
Former Congressman, Georgia,
Former Speaker of the House

"I believe personal strength is the most fundamental pillar of American civilization. It encompasses integrity, courage, hard work, perseverance, discipline, responsibility, and respect for others. Integrity is first and foremost, for it is at the core of freedom and at the core of a free society. Without integrity, the pillar crumbles, and with it the society."

John Glenn
Former Senator, Ohio; Astronaut

"If I am now considered a success it is not because I set out to become famous or successful, but because I always tried to do my very best at whatever I attempted. I feel much of my success has come from being at the right place at the right time with the preparation to take advantage of opportunity. I believe that commitment to ideals, respect for others, and serious study are essential for success in any field. The successful people I admire most are great readers, keen observers, and good listeners. They are curious and questioning about everything; not always trying to make things go their way, but striving to learn as much as they can and to understand how others see things. Most people, I believe, are capable of being successful if they choose worthwhile goals and prepare themselves for opportunities they will have."

Phil Gramm
Senator, Texas

"I failed the third, seventh and ninth grades, but my mother refused to give up on me. She had a dream that I would go to college, and she prodded me every step of the way. In America, a mother's dreams do not die easily, and I ultimately fulfilled my mother's dream by earning a Ph.D. in economics. The lesson taught by my mother's example and learned by me the hard way was simply that in our remarkable country, hard work and determination can overcome just about any obstacle."

Bill Graves
Governor, Kansas

"One of the most important aspects of a leader is his or her record of service. Being a great leader is not about gaining power—it is about working hard to provide timely, quality service to those whom you lead and to impact the lives of people around you in a positive manner. In the end, it is this record of service that people remember. Each day I try to do something to improve the lives of the people I serve."

Orrin G. Hatch
Senator, Utah

"It is an honor for me to be included among those who have distinguished themselves as members of our nation's armed forces both as recipients of the Congressional Medal of Honor and as POWs. You may not be aware that my only brother, a member of the Army Air Corps, was killed during WWII.

"A scripture that has always meant a great deal to me is Micah 6:8, 'He has shown you, O man, what is good; and what does the Lord require of you but to do justly, to love mercy, and to walk humbly with your God.'

"Like many people in politics, I have strong political views. Naturally, I think my views and values are right, and I have been known to fight hard for them. I would like to think that James Madison and I would be right in sync on the issues of today. But Micah reminds me of several things that are essential if we are to live as a free people under law. First, other people may be right too, and they are as entitled to their viewpoint as I am to mine. They are entitled to my respect even if I disagree with their proposals.

"Second, there is a difference between strongly held philosophical ideology and dogma. If we become dogmatic in our views, we may well shut out our justice and mercy. And, if dogma rules our lives and determines our every action, where is God? Have we begun to worship the dogma instead of God? We must strive to be true to our values; but we must also make sure that we do not sacrifice justice, mercy, or humility along the way."

Jesse A. Helms
Senator, North Carolina

"As I grew up in the small North Carolina town of Monroe in the 1930s, the idea of serving in the United States Congress—the world's most important legislative body—was beyond the imagination of a youngster to whom Washington and the federal government seemed a million miles distant. In late 1997, I completed my 25th year in the Senate.

"After all these years, I can still be moved to awe and to tears by the sight of the United States Capitol bathed in nighttime illumination. And I ponder the circumstances which led me to a seat in the same chamber where some of America's greatest men and women have debated and deliberated.

"What was responsible for the success I have been blessed with and attempted to use for the benefit of my country and my fellow men and women?

"There were many factors, of course, but the overriding factor was the 'still, small voice' which I was able to hear and heed. That voice has guided me since my early years. Its advice and counsel have always been available when I was in greatest need.

"God's voice and guidance are available to all who seek Him. Those that recognize His voice know that it will never lead them astray if they have true faith and abiding love for Him in their daily lives.

"God has led me to success in several careers, most notably during my years in the Senate. Whether or not my success has been accompanied by genuine significance is a question to be answered by others. I think that a person can live a life of significance without having attained success in terms of prominence, influence, and the acquisition of worldly goods. Conversely, many of the world's most outwardly successful people have provided little of beneficial significance to others.

"In my view, no person is successful, and no person's labors yield results of any significance, without the blessing of our heavenly Father. How vastly happier our planet and its inhabitants would be if all of us could get in touch with and abide by the guidance of the Lord who gave us life."

Mike Huckabee
Governor, Arkansas

"Leaders never ask others to do what they are unwilling to do. Leadership is more caught than taught. I believe the highest example of leadership was that of Jesus Christ, who personified a quality of leadership distinguished by servanthood and sacrifice. Real leadership is not getting behind people and kicking or coercing them into a certain action. It's getting in front of others and exhibiting a behavior that says, 'Follow me.' We should lead by loving, not shoving.

"The ultimate evaluation of effective leadership is not determined by how many people serve us, but rather how many people we serve."

Kenny Hulshof
Congressman, Missouri

"Four words I live by: *Sincerity*—constituents, like jurors, will rightly condemn the pretender; in all matters, they are owed the benefit of a sincerely-held opinion. Even the staunchest foe can appreciate the case presented by his adversary if the latter has brought honest reasoning to the debate.

Respect—It is foolhardy to render judgment after hearing only half the case. Such brashness invites intolerance. Every individual, regardless of station, has dignity and moral worth. True respect demands patience and reverence.

Humility—The best calisthenics that one can do is an exercise in humility. A victory is rarely achieved through a sole effort. Deflecting praise and accepting criticism—not the reverse—are hallmarks of the public servant.

Adversity—Most of this life's worthwhile lessons are ascertained through adversity. Thankfully, the Great Teacher provides comfort for us during our trails: 'Come to me, all you who are weary and find life burdensome, and I will refresh you. Take my yoke upon your shoulders and learn from me, for I am gentle and humble of heart. Your soul will find rest, for my yoke is easy and my burden is light'" (Matthew 11:28-30).

Asa Hutchinson
Congressman, Arkansas

"When I think of the principles that have guided me to where I am today, two come to mind: loyalty to one's personal beliefs and the persistence to stand up for those beliefs amidst opposition. However, I don't feel that my adherence to these two ideals make me stand out more than most.

"When I look back on all the people whose lives have been marked by success, these principles hold true to all. But most importantly, it is important to remember that success is not measured in worldly possessions or fame, but rather in the assuredness that you have remained true to your beliefs and have acted accordingly."

Mike Johanns
Governor, Nebraska

"No matter how many times people have tried to come up with one, and no matter how many books and magazines are written on the subject, the fact remains that there is no secret formula for a happy and successful life. In many ways, however, it is this unknown future that allows us to achieve our dreams. By charting our own path and finding our own formula for success, we are able to go beyond any preconceived notions about who we are and what we can do with our lives.

"I grew up the son of a dairy farmer in the heart of the rural Midwest. Since these early and cherished beginnings, more than I could have ever dreamed has come true in my life. I have had the privilege of serving the great people of the State of Nebraska as their Governor. I've sat with the President and the Vice President at the White House and talked about national policy. I've discussed the important issues of our day with other governors, ambassadors, foreign heads of state, and United States senators. My circle of friends extends world-wide, and I have made memories that will last a lifetime.

"But, after all of that, a few obvious and unmistakable truths remain that have guided my life throughout this journey and will guide my life to its end. First, honesty is not only the best policy, it is the very fabric that binds our relationships, both personal and professional, together. Second, civility, though very tough to find these days and especially in my line of work, should be the beacon that guides our life. Finally, family, faith, and commitment to your fellow man are the aspects of life that matter."

Gary E. Johnson
Governor, New Mexico

1. "Become reality-driven. Don't kid yourself or others. Find out what's what and base your decisions and actions on that.
2. Always be honest and tell the truth. It is extremely difficult to do any real damage to people who are willing to tell the truth, regardless of the consequences.
3. Always do what is right and fair. Remember, the more you

actually accomplish, the louder your critics become. Learn to ignore them. Maintain your integrity and continue to do what's right.

4. Determine your goal. Develop your plan to reach that goal, then act—don't procrastinate.

5. Make sure everyone who ought to know what you're doing, knows what you're doing.

6. Don't hesitate to deliver bad news. Acknowledge mistakes immediately. There may still be time to salvage things or to make corrections. Take Henry Kissinger's advice: 'Anything that will be revealed eventually should be revealed immediately.'

7. Be willing to do whatever it takes to get the job done. If your job doesn't excite you enough to follow the principle, resign and get a job you love enough to do what it takes."

Frank Keating
Governor, Oklahoma

"Life is about choices. We choose careers, mates, where to live, our recreational activities; but most of all, we choose how we will behave in our relationships with others and with God. Some of us make wrong choices at times; then, we either learn from them or continue to follow a path that brings us and those around us much misery. God gave us free will to make these choices, and I am convinced He wants us to make the right ones. Above all, we elevate ourselves and others when we make the truly difficult choices . . . those founded on a spiritual basis.

"Every human being knows the difference between right and wrong. We are all free to select our paths. When we make the right choices, we are in accord with what God wishes for us, and we are ultimately happy."

Steve Largent
Congressman, Oklahoma

"In the different roles I play—whether as a father, husband, boss, athlete, friend or Congressman—my love for Christ and His love for me, guides me. I have adopted 2 Chronicles 16:9 as my life verse. It says, 'For the eyes of the Lord range throughout the earth to strengthen those whose hearts are fully committed to him.' The first part of the scripture exemplifies God's tireless pursuit of a love relationship with us. The second part states clearly why God pursues a relationship with us—to strengthen us physically, spiritually, and emotionally. The last part lays out a prerequisite—we must be people whose hearts are fully committed to Him. We cannot serve two masters. God asks us for nothing less than our wholehearted and undivided devotion to Him. He deserves nothing less.

"In my role as a professional football player and as a United States Congressman, the majority of circumstances I encounter involve being a team player, working with a group of people to accomplish a common goal. Below are nine principles I share with my colleagues in the House of Representatives on the topic of 'Winning Together.'

1. Discipline
2. Trust
3. Accountability
4. There can be only one quarterback.
5. Common goal
6. Understand you can't plan for everything.
7. Prepare.
8. We're in a foxhole together.
9. Never forget that we are on the same team."

Richard Lugar
Senator, Indiana

"At the base of a hill in Granville, Ohio, which I used to climb to reach my alma mater, Denison University, are the words 'You shall know the truth and the truth shall make you free.'

"Increasingly, our nation lacks the zeal to search for the truth in public policy. Officials who consistently make unsound arguments often do so because they believe that their constituents do not want to find the truth which could adversely change their incomes, job prospects, and lifestyles. My charge to you is that you must develop your own capacities as truth seekers and truth tellers. The idea of searching for and then telling the truth as you found it is a difficult but not a new idea.

"Believe that God is listening to each word, and discipline your patterns of thought and speech accordingly. The ultimate, and most important, problem may be one of responsibility before God and eternity. An immediate problem is that lying destroys the human dignity of a person in addition to unraveling the code of conduct and confidence in which we are all bound by our assumptions that we are telling the truth to one another."

Connie Mack
Senator, Florida

"My brother, Michael, died in 1979 from melanoma. We struggled with the fight against that disease for 12 years. I can't begin to explain how Michael's struggle and death has touched my life. It was one of the most difficult things I've ever experienced, but what I learned from Michael can never be replaced.

"From Michael I learned many things. I learned it is not how old you become, but what you do with your life that is important. Make the most of every moment. I also learned that you should never give up. Until the very end, Michael never gave up. I couldn't believe his courage.

"Michael had read a book called *Gift From the Sea* by Anne Morrow Lindbergh, and one day he recommended that I read it. He thought it would help me get through the difficult times we were having. *Gift From the Sea* stressed the importance of understanding being alone—that it is in spending time alone that we stop being strangers to ourselves. It is in spending time alone that we can connect with our spiritual side and develop the inner strength that will help us with our lives, with our relationships with other people, and with our relationship with God."

Paul N. McCloskey, Jr.
Former Congressman, California

"An officer in the armed services is privileged, not ordained, to command troops. There is no essential formula for leadership. A quiet, humble person can provide it, as well as the strongest and most forceful of individuals. Competence, confidence, common sense, and compassion are as valuable as heroism and courage. Fear, and indeed terror, are understandable emotions when enemy fire is intense. No one need apologize for those feelings."

G.V. "Sonny" Montgomery
Former Congressman, Mississippi

"My code of conduct in life is pretty basic: Put your trust in the good Lord and don't hesitate to ask the Lord to help solve your problems.

"I try to treat others the way I would like to be treated. In my decisions of everyday life, I use common sense and honesty to come up with the right answers.

"Prayer and kindness have given me peace of mind."

Frank H. Murkowski
Senator, Alaska

"The best advice I can give to anyone is to strive to be ethical in every dealing, every day. Your wealth can dissipate, natural disasters can destroy your home, your health can deteriorate; but if you can maintain your good name and reputation, you will always be wealthy beyond measure.

"In this day and age, when press accounts might cause some to feel that honor is old-fashioned, I can think of nothing more important than for people to behave ethically, to keep their word and to follow their hearts. That is the best way to lay up your treasures in heaven, 'where moth or rust doth (not) corrupt, and where thieves (can't) break through and steal'" (Matthew 6:19).

Don Nickles
Senator, Oklahoma

"Seven steps to a better life:
1. Get up a half hour earlier than you normally do.
2. Get on your knees and have your quiet time. Express gratitude.

3. Read something positive—the New Testament, Psalms, Proverbs.
4. Go outside and look around. Breathe deeply and see the beauty. Meditate.
5. Get some exercise and take a quick shower.
6. Eat a good breakfast.
7. Greet everyone you see with love in your heart."

Lieutenant Colonel Oliver North, U.S. Marine Corps (Ret.)
National Security Council, Former Advisor

"Let me humbly commend to young officers the Roman Army Centurion in Matthew 8:5–13. The Roman officer (the equivalent of a Captain of Infantry) risks everything—his career, a court martial, perhaps even death by torture—for consorting with the well-known seditionist, Jesus Christ. And the Centurion takes these risks, not for his own advancement, promotion, or opportunity, but for one of his subordinates—probably a slave. There are many other lessons in those verses about the faith of that Centurion, but for young officers, no form of courage is greater than the act of self-sacrifice or personal jeopardy that they take for those they command."

Sam Nunn
Former Senator, Georgia

"Our problems in America today are primarily problems of the heart. The soul of our nation is the sum of our individual characters. Yes, we must balance the federal budget, and there are a lot of other things we need to do at the Federal level, but unless we change our hearts we will still have a deficit of the soul.

"The human inclination to seek political solutions for problems of the heart is nothing new. It is natural. Two thousand years ago, another society found itself in deeper trouble than our own. An oppressive empire strangled liberties. Violence and corruption were pervasive. Many of the people of the day hoped for the triumphant coming of a political savior, a long-expected king to establish a new, righteous government. Instead, God sent His son, a baby, born in a stable. Jesus grew up to become a peasant carpenter in a backwater town called Nazareth. He condemned sin but made it clear that he loved the sinner. He befriended beggars and prostitutes and even tax collectors while condemning the hypocrisy of those in power. He treated every individual with love and dignity and taught that we should do the same. He died like a common criminal, on a cross, and gave us the opportunity for redemption and the hope of eternal life."

Tom Osborne
Congressman, Nebraska

"As I have watched people grow and develop over the last 36 years of coaching, I have been impressed by the fact that our nation and our culture have undergone significant changes. Values that were taken for granted 20 or 30 years ago are no longer common, and young people are living in a very difficult time due to a deterioration of parental support and a progressive coarsening of the culture around them. It appears to me that a major spiritual awakening is very important to our nation at this time, since most great nations have fallen from *within* rather than have been conquered from *outside* forces.

"My faith has been very important to me and it has given me a compass and a rudder through some difficult times over many years of coaching. As the years have passed by, I have been more and more impressed by the goodness and greatness of God's grace. Oftentimes, it has been only in retrospect that I have seen decisions that I have made and people who have been placed in my life, as being providential rather than random or by chance events. These people have made all the difference in the direction my life has taken.

"The goal that has been most important in my life has been to attempt to honor God with what resources I have been given. At times, I have fallen far short of what I should have been, but with God's grace, hopefully I am living in a way that is somewhere closer to what He would have me be."

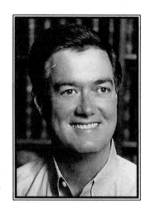

Bill Owens
Governor, Colorado

"The most important lessons I learned on moving from success to significance I learned from my father. My father passed away seven years ago, but not before spending a lifetime blessing me with his knowledge and experience and not before teaching me lessons every child needs to know.

"As a man, he taught me to be good, proud, honest, and above all, true to oneself and one's beliefs. As a door-to-door insurance salesman, he taught me the importance of hard work, congeniality, and perseverance. As a husband, he taught me to respect women, to treat them as equals. And as a father, he taught me the enormous impact unconditional love and support can have on a child's life. Not a day goes by that I don't think about him.

"The ethical and moral base with which I was provided as a child has carried me into adulthood and, working in the political arena where ethics and morals sometimes go by the wayside, I am blessed to be able to lean on that base.

"There are two Greek authors who perhaps summed up how best to lead an ethical and true life. The Greek poet Sophocles admonished, 'Rather fail with honor than succeed by fraud,' and the Greek sage Chilon said, 'Prefer loss to a dishonest gain; the one brings pain at the moment, the other for all time.'"

Paul E. Patton
Governor, Kentucky

"I have a positive outlook toward life. I believe it's filled with opportunities and challenges and the way to succeed is to be prepared for them. Education provides us with the tools necessary for life. Without education, it's much more difficult to enter the workplace, find a good job, and be able to provide a good quality of life for our families and ourselves. I also believe truly great leaders are those who care about people and are capable of making decisions that give everyone better lives and greater opportunities.

"I was fortunate to attend the University of Kentucky where I earned a degree in engineering. My mother worked as a cook, and I waited on tables to help pay for the degree. My parents always taught us that we need to open our lives to the accumulation of knowledge. With that college degree and my determination and drive, I've enjoyed success both in business and in public life. I know that without a good education, my loving family, and our faith in God, the future would not have been as bright."

Marc Racicot
Governor, Montana

"I would never presume to prescribe a Code of Conduct for anyone else. I would, however, list a few elements that I try to include in guiding my own conduct.

"We consistently try to do our homework on every issue; this involves studying all sides and their potential impacts. We try always to listen carefully. Every time I go to say something publicly, I ask myself if I have done all the listening I can. More often than not, I have not. We try to walk a mile in the moccasins of everyone we deal with. And we try to keep our eye on the ball; that is, our job is to help solve problems today. If we focus on today's problems today and tomorrow's problems tomorrow, then next year's opportunities will take care of themselves.

"Finally, I would add that my mother and my father (who was not only a basketball coach, he was MY basketball coach) instilled in every one of their seven children the instinct that we should never, ever, give up. I would not claim to live up to these goals every single instance in my 50 years, but getting closer is my target every single day."

Pat Roberts
Senator, Kansas

"I learned incalculable lessons from my experiences as an officer in the Marine Corps, as a Senator, and as a parent. In each of these roles, I have had to play the part of a leader. Whenever I am faced with a difficult decision or confronted with a complicated situation, I revert to the most basic principles in order to solve the dilemma. Leaders must approach problems with a determined work effort and a propensity for honesty. Strong character increases credibility and serves as the foundation for success."

Jim Ryun
Congressman, Kansas

"In the Fall of 1972, I just returned home from a heart-wrenching experience at the Munich Olympics where I had been tripped during the race and was subsequently unable to participate in the finals of the 1500 meters. A good friend of mine, Bernie Taylor, pinned to our front door a handwritten note with the words from Romans 5:3-5 (NIV).

Not only so, but we also rejoice in our sufferings, because we know that suffering produces perseverance; perseverance, character; and character, hope. And hope does not disappoint us, because God has poured out his love into our hearts by the Holy Spirit, whom He has given us.

"It was at this time that God began revealing to me that a man's character is forged through the fires of life and that character sustains and supports us through these fires. It is character, in the end, that gives us hope."

Edward Schafer
Governor, North Dakota

"There are two aspects of becoming successful that I feel are of great significance. First, hard work will enable you to move from being a dreamer to a dream maker. Anything is possible if you are willing to go the extra mile. Second, you must have faith. Jeremiah 29:11 (NIV) sums it up best by saying, 'For I know the plans I have for you,' declares the Lord, 'plans to prosper you and not to harm you, plans to give you hope and a future.' Hard work and faith are my personal creed and code of conduct, but I have gained some inspiring advice throughout my tenure in the public sector.

"To move from success to significance in the public sector, you must put the right people in place, let them know where you want them to go, and then get out of the way and let them get the job done! My political career has taught me that the politics of *politics* will get you elected, but the politics of *performance* will keep you there."

John M. Shimkus
Congressman, Illinois

"The following is my 'Citizens Code of Conduct.' I call it Shimkus' Citizen's Code of Conduct. It is modeled after the 'Military Code of Conduct.'

"I am an American citizen. I am blessed with this opportunity to live in a free, bountiful land. I accept the rights and responsibilities of citizenship.

"I will not allow the corrosive elements of cynicism, distrust, and hatred to destroy my feelings for my country. I will do all in my power to promote the good and welfare of the state and her citizens.

"The cornerstones of this great country are: faith in God, individual responsibility, and charity toward others. Even when assaulted by materialism, power, prestige and immorality, I will remember the God who made me and cares for me.

"I will play this game of life by the rules. I will not lie, cheat, or steal, nor will I tolerate those who do. I will lead by example, always building up my fellow citizens and not tearing them down.

"When I stumble, I will remember that this is America—the land of the free and the home of the brave, the land of endless opportunities. I will stay loyal to my forefathers who from the sweat of their brow became successful. I, too, will succeed.

"I will never forget that I am a United States citizen—responsible for my actions, and dedicated to the principles which made my country free. I will trust in my God and in the United States of America."

Cliff Stearns
Congressman, Florida

"I feel leadership is liberating people to do what is required of them in an effective manner. Therefore, a leader is a 'servant' of the people he manages. He is to encourage them and to use the strength of others to help the organization.

"The spirit of leadership is gentleness and self-control. Galatians 5:22-23, 'But the fruit of the Spirit is love, joy, peace, patience, kindness, goodness, faithfulness, gentleness, and self-control. Against such things there is no law.'"

Don Sundquist
Governor, Tennessee

"When I speak at college graduations, I try to pass along the following advice that has helped me along the way. It's simple advice, but I have found it to be invaluable.

- Life is a contact sport. The contacts you make with people will be as important as your job skills.
- If you expect to succeed, you have to be willing to take risks.

- The path is not always straight and smooth. Some will view the detours as obstacles, but try to see them as opportunities.
- Set ambitious goals, but keep in mind that life is as much about the journey as it is the destination. Whatever the destination, getting there is a great deal of fun and satisfaction.
- Have a sense of humor and keep things in perspective."

Jim Talent
Former Congressman, Missouri

"The search for significance begins with confronting the great, transcendent questions of life. Is there a God? Does He have a purpose for my life? How can I come to know Him and His plan for me? I found the answer to those questions in the death and resurrection of Jesus Christ. I urge everyone not to go through life so caught up in day-to-day tasks—as necessary as those tasks may be—without searching for the answer to these ageless questions. We can never be fully satisfied by even the good things in this life, because God put eternity in the hearts of men."

Fred Thompson
Senator, Tennessee

"At one time or another, all of us will find ourselves in the right place at the right time to assume leadership. Our job as individuals is to always be ready, for when that moment comes we must follow our conscience and do what's right. You never know who's looking to you for an example."

Strom Thurmond
Senator, South Carolina

"My advice to those who are interested in gaining leadership abilities begins with the values of honesty, integrity, and hard work. If you stand by these principles in everything you do, you can expect great rewards. In addition to honesty, integrity, and hard work, I encourage you to set high goals for yourself, especially where education is concerned. I believe that education is the golden door to opportunity, and you can never get too much education.

"The greatest satisfaction that I get from my work as a United States Senator comes from helping others. I have often said that my motto is 'helping others.' I urge you to volunteer in your school or community to help those who may benefit in some way from your interest and willingness to help. You may be surprised to experience the good feeling you get from simply helping others.

"To develop leadership I would offer this:

1. A leader must be honest.
2. Must have ability.
3. Must learn to think.
4. Must be a hard worker.
5. Must be courteous.
6. Must be courageous.
7. Must love people.
8. Must be cheerful.
9. Must learn to recognize and use the abilities of other people.
10. Must learn to organize.
11. Must put his trust in God."

Todd Tiahrt
Congressman, Kansas

"Reaching a point of 'significance' demands an extraordinary contribution from the mind, heart and soul. To fully seize the opportunity to make a difference in the world, in our families, or even in our own lives, we need a measure of patience because it takes more than just a willingness to do what is right. It takes time to create a desire for change in others and the ability to wait for God's perfect timing.

"In my own life, I have always had a desire to achieve. Coaches call it, 'the fire in the belly.' But as I grew older, I realized my desire for success had to be tempered with 'not just doing *a* thing right, but doing *the* right thing!' For those 'significant' decisions, I turn to my conscience which has been formed out of the wisdom passed on from my parents, grandparents, educators, friends, pastors, and of course, Sunday School teachers. Only then do I determine the right path to choose.

"Today, I strive for balance between the passion to right injustice, the knowledge I am but one man in the universe, and the love I have for my own family and my faith in God. Every time I look up at the United States Capitol, I say a little prayer, 'Lord, help me to do the right thing.' But in my desire to accomplish something of significance, I never forget the scripture passage found in Matthew 16:26 (NKJ): 'For what will it profit a man if he gains the whole world and loses his own soul.'"

James A. Traficant, Jr.
Congressman, Ohio

"A code of conduct or a creed is not just a policy concerning how we live our lives, but it is an attitude by which we live our lives in conjunction with other people. Throughout my life, I have witnessed situations where people were disrespected because of their race, financial condition, or simply because of their opinions. I have striven to treat others with respect, and to care about their concerns.

"The irony of my code of conduct or creed is that it is one that all of us have been taught and one that most of us forget. My code of conduct or creed is a common rule, the 'Golden Rule.' A simple rule to treat others with the same measure of respect that I would want them to treat me."

Tom Vilsack
Governor, Iowa

"My advice for life about both success and significance is: Grow your roots deep in the rich fertile soil of family and community, nourish your soul with faith and good works."

Zach Wamp
Congressman, Tennessee

"Before one becomes a real leader, one must first learn to serve. Today, our world looks at leadership in a narrow sense, but lasting leadership is demonstrated when a person has the commitment to others to be their servant first. By submitting him or herself to others, the leader gains their trust and support. The perfect model for leadership is Jesus Christ: whether you believe He is the Son of God or not, His life demonstrates my point very well. He washed the feet of the very people who were supposed to be His subjects. In service, we learn how to truly lead."

J.C. Watts, Jr.
Congressman, Oklahoma

"When it comes to the American dream, no one has a corner on the market. All of us have an equal chance to share that dream. In my wildest imagination, I never thought that the fifth of six children born to Helen and Buddy Watts—in a poor black neighborhood, in the rural community of Eufaula, Oklahoma—would someday be called 'Congressman.'

"Young people, America needs you. If our country is going to continue to be great, if it is going to continue to be strong, you are going to have to do your part. You are going to have to fight for America. Fight against skipping school and cheating on your papers. Fight against driving too fast and disobeying your parents. Fight against cursing and smoking. And fight, fight with every fiber of your being, against drugs and alcohol. You see, character *does* count. For too long, we have gotten by in a society that says the only right thing is to get by, and the only wrong thing is to get caught. Character is doing what's right when nobody is looking.

"The American Dream is about becoming the best you can be. It's not about your bank account, the kind of car you drive or the kind of clothes you wear. It's about using your gifts and abilities to be all that God meant you to be."

Frank R. Wolf
Congressman, Virginia

"What kind of men and women should we strive to be? I would refer you to the scripture, Micah 6:8 (NIV), 'He has showed you, O Man, what is good. And what does the Lord require of you? To act justly and to have mercy and to walk humbly with your God.' I challenge myself and I challenge you to follow these guidelines—to be a person who fears God, to be trustworthy, to be a person of integrity and character. We should ask ourselves: Do I want to be a person of excellence or a person of expedience? A person of principle or one who seeks to be popular? A person who looks for the right thing to do and does it, or one who finds the easy way around whatever I'm facing?"

PART V
RELIGIOUS AND SOCIAL LEADERS

"His gifts unto men were varied. Some he made messengers, some prophets, some preachers of the gospel; to some he gave the power to guide and teach people. His gifts were made that Christians might be properly equipped for their service, that the whole body might be built up" (Ephesians 4:11-12, Phillips).

Colonel E.H. Jim Ammerman
U.S. Army (Ret.)
Chaplaincy Full Gospel Churches, President

"INTEGRITY—acting the same as you talk—is the basis of character. FAITH—in God, through Jesus Christ, will keep us mindful that both God and I know if I'm always true. And the two of us are too many to know if I cheat. DILIGENCE—always giving my best will set me apart from the crowd; it is required of leaders. COURAGE—both moral and physical, are a must for leaders. We must, as military persons, be convinced that our mission is more important than our lives."

Gary Bauer
Family Research Council

"When I worked for President Reagan, I learned many things from him. One of the lessons that left a big impression on me was how much you could accomplish simply with the courage of your convictions. By sticking with what he knew was right, President Reagan made history by setting in motion the chain of events that eventually brought about the collapse of the Soviet Union. I remember that some people ridiculed the President for calling the

Soviet Union an 'Evil Empire.' But he knew he was right, and he didn't let the critics get to him. Instead, President Reagan set a course for victory in the cold war. His courage gave him the belief that we would prevail and that things would get better.

"That's a lesson I keep with me every day as I work to promote the pro-family agenda in our nation's capital. Here in Washington, it can be easy to get discouraged. The signs of cultural decay and the breakdown of the family are troubling. But I've learned to forget the naysayers and ignore the 'doom and gloom' crowd.

"America has always been a country that triumphed in the face of skeptics. Who could have predicted that a relatively small colonial outpost could take on the great British Empire and win? But we did. And every step of the way since, we've defied the odds. Hearty and brave, God-fearing and bold, Americans have tamed a great wilderness and brought free government to much of the world. And I'm convinced we can find our way out of our current troubles. The key is to know what you believe, stick with it, believe that things will get better, and never, ever give up.'"

Bob Boardman
Former missionary in Japan
Chaplain, Marine Corps Tanker's Association

"In Boot Camp, the first full day we were given that special, stylish Marine haircut, dungarees, and certain basic equipment. They also took our blood type, issued each man a serial number, and gave us a series of shots. This basic information was then stamped on two metal dog-tags which were to be worn around the neck day and night. My serial number was 506095—unforgettable! These two dog tags were as much a part of a Marine's career and persona as anything issued in the Corps. The only time they were to be removed was on the occasion of being either wounded in action (WIA) or killed in action (KIA)—two circumstances that you least desired in your still youthful life. But we were willing to take our chances in order to serve as Marines.

"Another vital piece of information that was stamped on our dog-tags was our religious affiliation. In WWII and the Korean War the designation was simple. If you were a Catholic, C was stamped right after your serial number, or P for Protestant, or H for Hebrew. If you were an atheist or agnostic, you drew a blank on your dog-tags. Good luck! I personally was a P at that time, simply because I wasn't a C or an H. I was a P in name only, stamped on metal.

"Shortly before taking that long train ride from Salem, Oregon, to San Diego, I was baptized at my parent's earnest request. But this good, traditional sacrament did not change the inside of my heart. My life remained as needy as ever, without inner peace or any type of hope, both in this life and also beyond the grave. If my name and number were to be called by the Grim Reaper, I was not ready to answer. I was only a dog-tag Christian.

"After an accelerated wartime Boot Camp of seven weeks, and then machine gun and tank training, we shipped out to Melbourne, Australia, to replace casualties in the First Marine Division of Guadalcanal fame.

"As we boarded ship, Red Cross workers gave each Marine a 'ditty' bag of personal items, one of which was a Gideon New Testament. A few weeks later in the little Australian town of Ballarat, while recovering from a severed tendon in my right wrist as a result of a drunken brawl, I began to diligently read that New Testament, seeking answers.

"In its pages I discovered that Jesus Christ loved me so much that He, the Son of God, had been willing to die on the Cross for all my sins—the fights, excessive drinking, using His name in vain, and all the rest. I learned about His resurrection from the dead which gave me hope beyond the grave.

"On Goodenough Island, near New Guinea in September, 1943, I accepted Jesus Christ as my Lord and Savior. He gave me heart-peace that transcends all human understanding. He helped me to move from being a dog-tag Christian to one upon whose heart Christ's name is stamped forever!

"I was severely wounded during the Battle of Okinawa. Shot in the throat, my voice and my life were changed forever. Following the war, I yielded to God's call to be a missionary. I was amazed that He directed me to Japan where I was a missionary for 33 years. Serve God wherever He calls you!"

Charles Brewster
National Director, Honor Bound:
Men of Promise

"Webster's dictionary defines complacent as, 'being satisfied.' As men, we can't be satisfied with our spiritual life. We should want more of God. We shouldn't become satisfied with what He has done, but look with expectant eyes for Him to guide our every move. If we keep looking back, we'll have a stale sense of God's presence in our lives, and we risk becoming complacent or 'lukewarm and spit out.'

"Overcoming complacency requires discipline. We must train ourselves to be subject to God and not flesh. It is a daily process. Physically, without exercise and proper diet, you become fat. The same is true spiritually; you must exercise daily with a steady disciplined diet in order to conquer 'Spiritual Flesh Fat.' Without training, spiritual fat will re-appear. Training requires daily sacrifice.

"The Bible says, 'Therefore I urge you, brothers, in view of God's mercy, to offer your bodies as living sacrifices, holy and pleasing to God—this is your spiritual act of worship' (Romans 12:1 NIV).

"Before God called me into ministry, I served as a Special Agent with the United States Secret Service for 23 years. I worked in law enforcement for a total of 28 years. I had been in training for many years to perform at my peak, so that lives could be saved.

"The Secret Service taught me to react contrary to human nature, to put myself between the person I was protecting and danger, standing literally 'in the line of fire.' Being able to become a shield when bullets are fired does not happen overnight. It takes discipline and training. The normal reaction is to 'get small' and take cover, not 'get large' and protect. Reacting to protect requires dedication to duty, consistent practice of reactions to real-life situations, conditioning yourself not to think before reacting, and reacting to your training. Training is the difference between life and death. Not yours, but the person you are sworn to protect.

"As believers, applying this training principle through the Word and Holy Spirit within us allows us to react to real-life situations according to the way God desires. In other words, training ourselves to react in line with His teaching. The daily sacrifices of spending time in the Word, prayer, worship, and fellowship are needed to prevent the 'Spiritual Flesh Fat' of the world from re-appearing in our lives. We will not and cannot be complacent when we submit to this discipline. This discipline develops 'expectant living.'

"Good advice to men would be: we must be clear-minded and self-controlled, so we can pray (I Peter 4:7 NIV), live godly lives (II Peter 3:10, 14, 17 NIV), become living sacrifices (Romans 12:1 NIV), pray in the Holy Spirit (Jude 18:23 NIV), and become holy because He is holy (I Peter 1:13-16 NIV). We don't need to 'do' church; we need to be the church. We need to die to ourselves and live for Jesus."

David Brickner
Executive Director, Jews for Jesus

"Many people view opposition and difficulty as an indication that something is wrong or that they are moving in the wrong direction. I have found just the opposite to be true. Anything that's worth doing in this life will require some measure of sacrifice and undoubtedly incur some measure of opposition. In Jews for Jesus, we often measure our success by the level of opposition we are experiencing. If we have no opposition, it often means that people aren't paying attention to what we're trying to say.

"Some of the greatest leaders throughout history have been known as much by the opposition they had to overcome as by the success they achieved. Time and time again, I have found in my life that opposition can be transformed in an opportunity to stand for God and accomplish more than you ever dreamed possible. When you experience opposition, meet it head on, stand firm, and look for the opportunity to make your life count."

Bill Bright
Founder and President,
Campus Crusade for Christ International

"Our Lord gave one major prerequisite to leadership—servant-hood. In a somewhat amusing encounter, one day the mother of Zebedee's sons came to Jesus and asked that He promote her sons to sit at His right and left hands in the kingdom. When 'the ten' heard about this, they were indignant. This triggered a response from the Lord that is the greatest leadership principle ever given. He said: 'You know that the rulers of the Gentiles lord it over them, and their high officials exercise authority over them. Not so with you. Instead, whoever wants to become great among you must be your servant, and whoever wants to be first must be your slave—just as the Son of Man did not come to be served, but to serve, and to give his life as a ransom for many' (Matthew 20:25-28 NIV).

"In modern corporate vernacular, the Lord would say, 'Look, here's the way it works in my organization. The key to getting ahead is to serve. The greater servant you become, the more you will be promoted.' And what an example He set! The Creator laid aside all His glory to come down to Earth to serve mere humans."

Bob Buford
The Buford Foundation
Author, Halftime and Game Plan

"In my mid 40s, earning a lot of money and growing my business did not give me the satisfaction it once did. The increasing turmoil over the direction of my life led me to a strategic business consultant. The most piercing question the consultant asked me was, 'What's in the box?' Then he became more specific—'I've been listening to you for over two hours and I can't help you unless you put one thing into the box. For you, it is either money or Jesus Christ.' He asked me to draw a square on a piece of paper and then place a symbol inside the box that represented my life's central passion. One symbol. One passion. I had to choose.

"Taking a deep breath, I reached for my pen, and drew a little cross in the middle of the box I had sketched on my legal pad. By doing that, I was saying to God, 'I'm yours. From now on, nothing will be as important to me as You.' It is never easy to say a complete 'yes' to Christ. I admit that drawing the little cross in the box was scary. But God has let me be what He created me to be—an entrepreneur. I still enjoy the thrill of forming deals, but now it's in another context—instead of buying cable television systems, I am creating new ventures to help other successful people turn their faith into action.

"When you place Christ in your life's box, you will embark on an enormous adventure that will be more fulfilling than any worldly success. You are on the journey from success to significance."

Larry Burkett
Christian Financial Concepts

"The principles God has given us to live by in His Word are neither complicated nor harsh. In fact, they are designed to free us of a set of rigid do's and don'ts. The difficulty is that so many American families have adopted get-rich quick mentalities that even the way they buy basic necessities has been affected. God's principles of financial management have been largely ignored for the last 40 years, and now we are reaping what has been sown.

"A case in point: One of the largest mail order companies in the country decided to go out of business, despite the fact that sales were higher that ever. However, so were nonpayments from their sales force: children who were being supplied seeds to sell door-to-door. The nonpayment rate had risen steadily since the 60s, until by 1991 it reached 70 percent. The final straw came when the company attempted to contact parents, in hopes they would help in collection, only to discover they were actually encouraging the kids to keep the company's money.

"In this case, the symptom was nonpayment of a legitimate debt, but the problem went much deeper, involving basic values that parents no longer teach their children. It's vitally important for parents to realize that their own personal integrity will be reflected in the lives of their children. As parents walk in biblical integrity as responsible adults, their children will tend to follow in their footsteps. 'A righteous man who walks in his integrity; how blessed are his sons after him' (Proverbs 20:7)."

John Busby
National Commander, The Salvation Army

"Greatness comes from placing one's faith and values on the solid foundation of the revealed Word of God. The place to start is in affirming the great confession. It was a significant moment in Christ's teaching of his disciples when Peter proclaimed, 'You are the Christ, the Son of the Living God' (Matthew 16:16). It's the starting place for all of us.

"When questioned regarding which was the greatest commandment in the law, Jesus was quick to answer, 'Love the Lord your God with all your heart, with all your soul, and with all you mind...love your neighbor as yourself.' (Matthew 22:37-39) Modeling the great commandment is clearly proclaimed as basic in who we are to be.

"Christ's final admonition to those he was teaching was, 'Go and make disciples of all nations...teaching them to obey everything I have commanded you' (Matthew 28:19-20). Advancing the great commission clearly portrays what it is we are to do. Greatness comes not through what we gain for ourselves, but in aligning our lives in pursuit of what God recognizes as great."

Tony Campolo
Professor, Eastern College
Founder, President, EAPE/Kingdomworks

"When I was a teenager I read the book, *In His Steps*, by Charles Sheldon. I decided then to commit myself to doing whatever Jesus would do if Jesus was in my place and in my situation. There are many sophisticated courses in personal and societal ethics that one could study, but in the end, I believe that my life has boiled down to the simple formula of trying to understand what Jesus would do, and then committing myself to doing it.

"As I look at my life, and I ask what it all has meant, I have to conclude that in the end it has been those things that I have done for the poor and the oppressed that have given me significance. Recognition by society is a very fleeting thing, and the wealth and the power that can be accumulated through life's achievements soon pass away. What we do for what the Bible call 'the least of the brothers and sisters' has enduring significance. The Bible says in the 25th chapter of Matthew that what we have done for those who are hungry, naked, sick, imprisoned, and lonely will be what matters when we are judged on that final day."

Michael Cassidy
Founder, African Enterprise

"My creed is simple: Jesus Christ is God, Lord, Savior of humankind, and coming King; from that flows my code of conduct and the path from success to significance.

1. Hand everything over to Him, stay His friend, and be true to Him.
2. Stand firm on the Bible as God's authoritative guide for life and living.
3. Aim to correlate behavior to profession but rejoice in God's forgiveness for failure.
4. Be always willing to tell others about the One whom to know is life eternal.
5. Keep all life's primary relationships strong and intact, for this is the heart of things.
6. Discern God's place and calling for life and stay at the center of His will.
7. Give everything your best shot.
8. Make forgiveness a way of life and do not retaliate for wrongs inflicted, because vindication of His own is God's business.
9. Be strong and very courageous, as God told Joshua, because life is tough, but it yields to courage.
10. Aim to finish better than you started, remembering too that when this day is done, the best is yet to be, because heaven is our final home."

Edwin Louis Cole
Christian Men's Network

"Probably the only strength I have ever had in life is that of being a lover of the truth. Truth is the foundation for the way you live and the life you have. A foundational truth upon which my life has been built is that when you prove yourself faithful in that which belongs to another, you become qualified to have your own. Where I have been unfaithful at any time, to anyone, or anything, I have tried to be faithful to ask forgiveness. It has allowed me to live with a good conscience toward God and men."

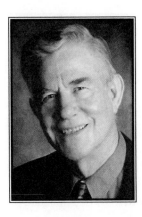

Robert E. Coleman
Trinity Evangelical Divinity School

"When Jesus said, 'Follow me,' He not only set a new direction in my life; He established a new way of leadership that captivated my heart. Not like an indulgent manager, He leads like a shepherd-one who loves his sheep and lays His life down for them.

"Jesus reverses the value of this world, and in so doing, redefines the meaning of significance. By this standard, greatness comes through servanthood, and success through a cross. To use His words, 'Whoever wants to save his life will lose it, but whoever loses his life for me will find it.' (Matthew 16:25)

"This is the path I have chosen. Though my own faltering obedience falls infinitely short of my Savior's example, in following Christ I have found a fullness of joy and peace the world can not take away, and I know that the best is yet to be."

Charles Colson
Prison Fellowship Ministry

"There have been two great character-forming experiences in my life. The first was the Marine Corps which taught me duty, gave me confidence in my abilities to be a good Marine, and taught me about loyalty. *Semper Fidelis* was not only my creed as a Marine Officer but has served me well through the rest of my life.

"The second character forming experience was far more important. I met Jesus Christ as my Lord and Savior in the summer of 1973 in the midst of the Watergate scandal. But the Lord sustained me when I went from the office next to the President of the United States to a prison cell. And He has sustained me ever since in my ministry.

"The creed of the Corps is a pretty good guide for life. Duty is a forgotten word in today's culture. The Marine knows duty because his life is committed to doing it in the service of his country. We do it out of gratitude to those who went before us and defended the liberties we enjoy today.

"All the more does the Christian understand duty which was called by a great Christian writer once 'the mother of all virtues.' Out of gratitude to God for what He did through His Son Jesus Christ on the cross, taking away my sins, I can do no less than to serve Him with all my life, that is to do my duty as a Christian. *Semper Fidelis*, always faithful, is a second worthy creed. My loyalty has been at times misplaced—one should never be loyal to less than a totally honorable cause. But loyalty as a Christian can never be misplaced. We are loyal to Christ and we show our loyalty by living in totally faithful obedience to His commands."

Craig Conrad
Christian Military Fellowship, Executive Director

"As a Christian, I've made it my goal in life to live under the direction of the Lord Jesus Christ who teaches us to love God with all our hearts, souls and minds and to love our neighbors as ourselves (Matthew 22:37-40). So in response to His love and reliance upon His grace, I purpose to follow Him (John 14:15). Therefore, I try, in accordance with what is called the 'Golden Rule' (Luke 6:31), to do or not do unto others that which I would be willing to have done or not done unto me or anyone else. Consequently, my creed or code of conduct can be summarized as 'LOVE GOD, LOVE PEOPLE.'

"It has been my experience that successful people are those who know what they are doing and do it well, stay on task, and live with integrity. So success, as I think it is usually understood, is a function of competence and character that is rewarded by increasing responsibility, as well as the prerogatives of power and privilege.

"But significant people are those who, rather than cling to the privileges of success, use the powers thereof to serve the best interest of others. I therefore believe that moving from success to significance requires us to LEARN HUMILITY.

"'Do nothing out of selfish ambition or vain conceit, but in humility consider others better than yourselves. Each of you should look not only to your own interests, but also to the interests of others. Your attitude should be the same as Christ Jesus, Who being in very nature God, did not consider equality with God something to be grasped, but made Himself nothing, taking the very nature of a servant, being made in human likeness. And being found in appearance as a man, He humbled Himself and became obedient to death—even death on a cross!'" (Philippians 2:3-8, NIV)

Kenneth Copeland
Kenneth Copeland Ministries

"A very wise man once told his son, 'Attend to my words; incline thine ear unto my sayings. Let them not depart from thine eyes; keep them in the midst of thine heart. For they are life unto those that find them...' (Proverbs 4:20-22).

"To incline thine ear simply means, 'be ready to hear God—and be ready to change.'

"Let's face it, God is a lot smarter than we are. We are the ones who need to be making changes. We need to be ready to change what we think, how we feel, what we say. We need to be ready to change anything that doesn't line up with His Word.

"If there's anything I've learned in 34 years of ministry, it's this: Put God's Word first place in your life and make it final authority. Do whatever it tells you to do—pray, listen, and obey—and you'll know more success and more significance than you ever imagined possible in this life."

Lawrence J. Crabb
Institute of Biblical Counseling

"There is a mystery about life that can never be reduced to human explanation. Why did this tragedy happen? Why is this person I care about moving in such terrible directions? In these areas of life, resist the strong passions to explain and control. Let the unexplainable drive you to trust. In realms we cannot see, a larger story is being told. Ask only what God has called you to do, what talents He has given to you to use, what opportunities He provides for you to serve His purposes. Then go for it. The courage to move ahead in the darkness of mystery is central to knowing fulfillment. Never take responsibility for what you cannot control but take full responsibility for everything God has called you to do. The next step will always be illuminated to the courageous."

Nicky Cruz
Nicky Cruz Outreach

"My life, although simple, started with a complicated beginning. I had no hope and I never believed there would ever be hope. As a young boy I was involved in a life of violence and gangs. When

I came to know Christ, I was transformed by a life-changing 'born again' experience. My life moved from hopelessness and disdain for life to an appreciation of life.

"When I look at myself and analyze the 'success' I have experienced, I realize it was not me that accomplished anything. From an early age, I was embraced by failure. I never really knew that God had given talents to me.

"There are many people in the same situation. They are in the very 'gutter' of life and will never discover or become aware of their God-given talents. Many have died and will die and never discover they have been given a gift. I was blessed, someone came to me in that gutter and told me that there is a God, a Man—Jesus Christ, the Savior. Jesus Christ saw people in need and he felt their pain and suffering. From His willingness to touch hurting people and to feel their suffering, I have learned to have eyes to see and a heart to feel their pain also.

"In life you can accomplish great things. You can have many earthly possessions, yet be spiritually bankrupt. In gaining material success, you can, ironically, lose it all. Success, once achieved, lasts but a moment. You need something to give success meaning. Character and integrity are the essence of who you are and help determine true success. Real character, real integrity, comes from Christ.

"Significance is the inheritance, the legacy, that you leave your family and society. The significance I am referring to is not monetary. Some believe that success and significance are the same. They are not. A person can be a success, even accomplish great things, yet they are failures with their family, with 'friends,' and with God.

"In my life, God is number one, then family, and then friends. That's the way I set my priorities. The desire that I have for my family is that they take possession of what I value, and what I value is a relationship with the Lord Jesus Christ."

Ken Davis
Dynamic Communications

"My father is an ex-POW and a survivor of the Bataan Death March. During his captivity he saw perfectly healthy men die because they had no reason to live. They gave up hope. He also saw men who were at death's threshold live to be liberated and enjoy long, healthy lives. These men had a reason to live.

"Years ago I saw a picture in which a young man carried a sign that said: 'Nothing is worth dying for.' Until a man or woman finds a purpose worth dying for, they will never have a purpose to live for. My father and thousands like him shed blood so I might live in freedom. My Father in heaven did the same thing. When I least deserved it, God gave His Son so that I might be freed from the penalty of my own sin.

"My code of conduct is this: To live every day to honor the sacrifice that was made for my life and to be prepared at any moment to die for that same cause.

"Philippians 1:20-21 (NIV): 'I eagerly expect and hope that I will in no way be ashamed but will have sufficient courage so that now as always Christ will be exalted in my body, whether by life or by death. For to me, to live is Christ and to die is gain.'"

James Dobson
Founder, Focus on the Family

Dr. Dobson offers this advice from his book *What Wives Wish Their Husbands Knew About Women* by Tyndale House Publishers. "I have concluded that the accumulation of wealth, even if I could achieve it, is an insufficient reason for living. When I reach the end of my days, a moment or two from now, I must look backward on something more meaningful than the pursuit of houses and land and machines and stocks and bonds. Nor is fame of lasting benefit. I will consider my earthly existence to have been wasted unless I can recall a loving family, a consistent investment in the lives of people, and an earnest attempt to serve the God who made me. Nothing else makes much sense."

Phil Downer
President, Christian Business Men's Committee

"I make no apologies: I want to change the world. The most effective way to change the world is to reach others with the saving message of Jesus and reproduce myself in them. All Christians can make an eternal impact in the lives of others if we allow God to use us for His purpose.

"When I was in Vietnam, I was a soldier on the front lines, equipped for battle. I did not want to wait around in the rear area. The Marines had trained me to fight, and that's what I wanted to do. I feel the same way about my faith. Believers have not been called to sit in the barracks, or to hide behind the lines, or to pretend we are not in the army of God..

"I want to leave a legacy of trained, active spiritual soldiers of the cross, who stand in the gap for the Lord Jesus Christ, winning and discipling others long after I am gone. My own children can make an eternal impact on the world by my shaping them into soldiers for the cause for Christ, so that the vision God has planted in my life will continue to grow through my kids."

Dave Dravecky
Outreach of Hope

Dave offered the following advice about success and significance reprinted from his book *The Worth of A Man*, Zondervan Publishing House. "A few months after I lost my left arm and shoulder, I had to face some difficult questions. All my life I had trained and practiced and sacrificed and sweat to become a major league ballplayer, and I had made it. Then, at the height of my career, cancer took it all away from me. Life forced me to ask gut-level questions such as these: Who am I? What will I do now? Without my pitching arm, what am I worth? If my worth doesn't come from baseball, where does it come from?

"I knew that a left-handed pitcher without a left hand wasn't 'worth' anything to a major league ball club—not as a pitcher, anyway, and that's all I ever wanted to be. So now I had to answer a huge question to which I had previously never given much thought: What is Dave Dravecky worth, not as a baseball player, but as a man? And where does that worth come from?

"So what is a man worth, especially a Christian man? What is he worth when everything about him is stripped away except for his very self? What is a man worth apart from his relationships or his ability to work and create? When a man stands naked before God, with nothing in his hands and no one at his side, what is he worth?

"I am discovering that our worth as men is far beyond measurement solely because of what God has done for us and in us. Our worth stems not from what we have or what we do or what we control or whom we know, but from what God has done for us and in us. That was great news to me, because I always felt (regardless of what I said) that my worth stemmed from my performance—if I performed well, I was worth a lot; if I messed up, I wasn't worth much. But when I finally started to discover that my worth wasn't tied even a little to my abilities or my performance, but rather depended entirely and forever in what God already had done in and for me, my world suddenly opened up. I was free!"

Rabbi Yechiel Eckstein
International Fellowship of Christians and Jews

- "Strive for completeness of 'shalom' within our selves, with God and with our family and friends. Let God's peace and wholeness imbue all our relationships.
- Strive toward holiness with God, others, and the world.
- Love your fellow man. Remember, God's spirit is in them, too.
- Be humble. Yes, above all else, be humble. And let God's will become your own way of living.
- Be grateful every moment of every day and remember to seize every moment of every day.

despair from striving to bring redemption, peace, and an
ɔ suffering in the world.

- ~~~. ever give up the dream of the way the world ought
  to be...and can be, with our input.
- Don't ever forfeit life to those who seek to expel God's presence
  from the world rather than bring Him into it.
- Love God 'with all your heart, all your soul, and all your might.'
- Teach these lessons 'to your children, and speak of them when
  you dwell in your home, walk on the way, when you lie down,
  and rise up.'
- Be humble. Yes, above all else, be humble."

Anthony T. Evans
President, The Urban Alternative
Pastor, Oak Cliff Bible Fellowship

"The moral fabric of America is being torn to shreds by issues
such as family disintegration, crime, racial division, injustice, and
countless other problems that are destroying our culture. The core
cause of the problems we face is a spiritual one; therefore, the only
successful way to address these issues is spiritually. You can only
change society when you change the human heart, and the only
way to effect lasting change in the human heart is through a life-
changing relationship with Jesus Christ."

Jerry Falwell
Founder-Pastor, Thomas Road Baptist Church

"As a code of conduct, I would tell a person first, give yourself to Jesus Christ and become a Christian. This will give you the assurance that upon death you would go to heaven.

"Second, I would tell a person to surrender completely to Jesus Christ, and let Him be the Lord of your life. You do this by praying daily, 'Not my will but Thine be done.'

"Third, I would say to every person that they should meet God early each morning, whereby they read the Word of God (getting direction from God), pray to God (sharing one's needs and desires with God), and in that quiet time of meditation with the Lord, get strength to serve God each day.

"Fourth, conscientiously obey all the principles found in scripture, attempting to live in the power of Christ and to live for Christ.

"Fifth, be active in a local church, where you fellowship with others, pray, sing, give your offerings, and serve God. By living for a cause greater than yourself, you will gain emotional strength and a purpose in life, so that you can glorify God.

"Sixth, be a committed family man or family woman. The most important person in life is your spouse where you build up one another in Christ.

"Seventh, be a loving parent, raise your children to love and serve God.

"The key verse that I would give to a person as a code of conduct is, 'For me to live is Christ, and to die is gain'" (Phil. 1:21).

Steve Farrar
Men's Leadership Ministries

"My creed, my code of conduct for life is, 'You shall love the LORD your God with all your heart, with all your soul, and with all your strength' (Deuteronomy 6:5 NKJ). When a man loves God from his gut it affects every single area of his life and every decision of his life. A man who lives his life to please God will be a man of integrity and conviction in every area of his life.

"How do you move from success to significance? 'And these words which I command you today shall be in your heart. You shall teach them diligently to your children, and shall talk of them when you sit in your house, when you walk by the way, when you lie down, and when you rise up (Deuteronomy 6:6-7 NKJ). A man moves from success to significance when he has the vision to transfer the truth of God from his own heart to the next generation. That's how a man moves from success to significance. He transfers the truth in his own life to his children by living out the truth of God before them.

"Reputation is what people think you are. Character is what you are when no one else is around. A true leader does not separate his private life from his public life. What a man is in private is what he will ultimately be in public. A man can fool the public, but he cannot fool his children. And when they see the truth of God in his own life, his children will be very prone to emulate the model and example of their father. That is significance."

Bruce Fong
Professor, Multnomah Biblical Seminary

"The driving force in my life is the following: 'Stand firm. Let nothing move you. Always give yourselves to the work of the Lord, because you know that your labor in the Lord is not in vain' (I Corinthians 15:58 NIV). Leaders must know with certainty their mission and be passionate in carrying it out. Faith, trust, belief are essential in fulfilling any task at hand. As a servant of God, I devote myself tirelessly to His service. In the process, I keep focused with the following motto: 'Do one thing profoundly and everything else well.' I minister based upon the strengths and gifts that God has entrusted to me and by His Spirit attempt to grow in all areas that are related to serving for His glory."

E. Bernard Franklin
Vice President, Urban Director, National Center
for Fathering

"I remember early in my childhood, during the preteen and early teen years, I had a profound fascination with the writings of Paul. I read and re-read Philippians 3:10 (NIV). Paul described his strong desire 'to know Christ and the power of His resurrection and the fellowship of sharing in His sufferings, becoming like Him in His death, and somehow, to attain the resurrection from the dead.' I am sure as a child I did not understand this verse as Paul intended it, but it meant a lot to me.

"I grew up with a distant, angry father who did not let his children really know him. Perhaps I was so taken with Paul's desire to know Christ because it was my deep personal desire to really 'know' my father. Nonetheless, I was moved by Paul's desire to know Christ, and I prayed that prayer on many days.

"Now as an adult, I have come to see that the person I wanted to know was working on my behalf to cement my desire to know Him, even then, in difficult, painful, and hard times. I have come to see that it has been my desire to know Christ which has sustained me through many challenges as an adult. I am convinced that I would not be where I am today had Christ not placed in my heart as a child the desire to know Him 'and the power of his resurrection and the fellowship of His sufferings.'

"I am of the opinion that the Church today spends a great deal of time helping folks avoid 'the fellowship of His sufferings.' As a result, many people do not want to suffer through the challenges of living in this life and in so doing they forsake the wonderful fellowship with the Savior. I believe the need of the hour is for men to desire nothing more than to know the personality and power of the Savior of the world, and for men to wrestle until that knowing is satisfied."

Bill Glass
Bill Glass Ministries

"I don't have enough faith to be an atheist. It takes a lot of faith to be an atheist. You have to believe that 'No one X Nothing + Blind Chance = Everything' and when I look at the billions of galaxies in space, I am amazed with the immensity and the perfection of the universe.

"We live in a galaxy called the Milky Way. If you could travel at the speed of light (186,000 miles per second) for 100,000 years, you would get across the Milky Way one time. But they discovered a galaxy several years back by the name of Markian 348, and it would take 13 times longer to get across Markian 348. In other words, it would take 1,300,000 years to get across Markian 348. Only recently they discovered, by the use of the Hubbell Telescope, a galaxy called Abel 2029. Abel 2029 is 65 times bigger than Markian 348. We've only discussed three galaxies and there are literally billions of galaxies. Do you feel small? I do!

"If I had 10 pennies in my pocket, numbered 1 through 10, and I wanted to pick those 10 pennies out of my pocket in succession, the odds that I could pick out penny number 1 are 1 in 10. The odds that I could pick out penny number 1 and 2 are 1 in 100. The odds that I could pick out pennies 1 through 3 are 1 in 1,000. The odds that I could pick out pennies consecutively numbered 1 through 10 are 1 in 10 billion. In other words, don't bet on it. It's a bad bet.

"If you bet against God, you make an infinitely worse bet because you're betting that you and I and the whole universe are just one great big super colossal accident. The movement of the stars is so precise that we even correct our clocks by it. Anything that big that moves that precisely has to have a creator. Just like you wouldn't expect an accidental watch or car, neither would you expect the universe to be accidental.

"My first guiding principle is 'Don't bet against God. It's a dumb bet!' My second guiding principle is "The infinite value of the soul.' Christ said, "What shall it profit a man, if he gain the whole world and lose his soul? Or what shall man give in exchange for his soul.' The way you determine the value of a thing is to know who made it. You can see a violin and think that because it's in terrible condition, it's not worth very much. But if you discover that it's a Stradivarius, then you know it has great value.

"If you see a painting and you're unimpressed, but then you discover Rembrandt painted it, then you realize it is worth a lot. 'Then the Lord God formed man of the dust from the ground and breathed into his nostrils the breath of life, and man became a living soul' (Genesis 2:7). We were made by God. We are of great worth because God, the Creator of all things, is our Maker. He designed us, made us; we are precious, and our soul is extremely valuable. The reason some people act like animals is because they don't realize the great value of the soul.

"The second way you determine the value of anything is by its complexity. Man is infinitely complex. God created man in His own image. This does not speak of the physical creation; God is not a physical being. So it means that He created us to be spiritually like Him—in His spiritual image. You must say aloud, 'I am a magnificent person! Eternal God makes me in His image. Everything God makes is great and I am the height of His creation, because I'm like Him. I am God's best work, the supreme creation. I and every other human being have the potential for fellowship with Him because I am, because we are made in His likeness.'

"Since I am in wonderment of the terrific value of the human soul, it gives me great respect for myself. And even greater concern about the eternal souls of those that are around me. It is impossible to love our neighbor if we don't love ourselves. When we're struck with the great love that God has for us, in that He created us with eternal souls, then we also are struck with the importance of the souls and of others, and we reach out to them in love and compassion.

"We find significance in losing ourselves in service to Christ and others. And to the degree that we become self-centered, thinking only of our own well-being and not of others, we become introverted and even depressed. But when we reach out to others in compassion and love, then we discover great joy and true significance."

Geoff Gorsuch
The Navigators/The National Coalition of Men's Ministries

"I learned the essence of my code of conduct while leading fighters into combat as an OV-10 'Nail' (Forward Air Controller) in Vietnam. Having authority over men and their war machines in a 'kill or be killed' situation, I realized that the key to victory was having one eye on the objective while the other eye was always on the men. I had to care—really care—for them. It took time, effort and energy to get the pilots safely 'home.' But, by God's grace, we did.

"Ever since, I measure 'success' not only by the goals achieved, but by how many men were helped along the way. Jesus said that the 'heart' of leadership was 'not to be served, but to serve and to give your life,' for those you are leading. He ultimately did. And as a veteran, I saw how worthy Jesus' example was. Then, as a husband and father, I saw its value again. And now as a leader in Christian missions, I've seen it proved time and again all over the world: the true leader is a servant. By God's grace he's learned to put the well-being of others ahead of personal ambition. And as he does, he's given greater opportunity to model the heart of a true leader."

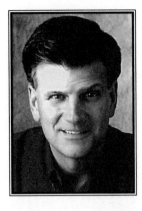

Franklin Graham
President, Samaritan's Purse

"Do you regard prayer as one of your top priorities for each day? Jesus did. God's Word tells us that prayer was central in the earthly life and ministry of our Lord. 'Now in the morning, having risen a long while before daylight, He went out and departed to a solitary place; and there He prayed' (Mark 1:35, NKJV).

"Jesus had been busy the previous night healing the sick, but He got up before daybreak the next morning to spend time in prayer. When it is hard for us to find time to pray, we need to make time to talk with God—even if we have to get up early to do it.

"'So He Himself often withdrew into the wilderness and prayed' (Luke 5:16). Even when the multitudes were clamoring for His attention, Jesus made it a point to find a quiet place to pray. With all the things that clamor for our attention—phone calls, appointments, deadlines, errands—we may think we are too busy to pray. In reality, we are too busy not to pray. We can accomplish so much more when our work is grounded in prayer."

Billy Graham
Evangelist, Billy Graham Evangelistic Assn.

"Be faithful in whatever place God puts you. Pace your life according to the will and plan of God for you. You are yet young, and you have only begun to see what God can do through a life that is dedicated to Him. Do not become impatient, or try to go on ahead of God. His track record is without failure, while our efforts can only end in frustration. Be determined to live your life with Jesus Christ at the center, enjoying daily times of prayer and Bible study. Be sure that you share your faith regularly, and trust God to lead you step by step in a life that is totally yielded to Him."

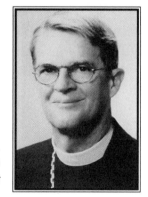

Frank T. Griswold
Presiding Bishop, Primate, Episcopal Church in the United States

"My advice would be to develop the life of the spirit, the interior life, where we are put in touch with the Christ within. Because Jesus Christ is the incarnate and glorified Word of God, fundamental to all spirituality is the capacity and willingness on the part of persons of faith to listen. 'Oh that today you would harken to His voice!' says Psalm 95.

"This discipline of listening also applies to the words of those persons around us: those with whom we agree, and also those with ideas different from our own. Each of us has a piece of God's truth. Each of us is a limb on the Body of Christ. Together we serve our Lord, each offering a different gift. If we keep this in mind, we honor our diversity rather than finding it divisive."

Richard L. Hamm
General Minister and President, The Christian
Church (Disciples of Christ)

"The ancient Hebrew prophet, Micah, wrote, 'What does the Lord require of you, O mortal, but to do justice, love kindness and walk humbly with your God.' As I live out my life and ministry, these are words that have guided me. 'Doing justice' means doing whatever we can to see to it that everyone has a fair opportunity in life. This means combating racism, sexism, classism, and any of the evils that dehumanize people and limit their opportunity to live a full and meaningful life.

"'Loving kindness' means practicing the Golden Rule: 'Do unto others as you would have them do unto you.' 'Walking humbly with God' means recognizing that I am less than perfect, that I often fail morally and otherwise and am utterly dependent on the grace of God and God's forgiveness. When I remember that God forgives me every day, I am better able to forgive those who offend or hurt me. I commend these three guideposts to you. 'Do justice, love kindness, walk humbly with your God.'"

Howard Hendricks
Chairman, Center for Christian Leadership
Dallas Theological Seminary

"The greatest crisis in America today is a crisis of leadership. The greatest peril of leadership is a crisis of character.

"A man of integrity has nothing to hide. He has nothing to fear. He has nothing to prove. And he has nothing to lose except his wholeness and integrity.

"Proverb 20:7, one of my favorites, reads, 'The righteous man walks in integrity; his children are blessed after him' (NKJ). The greatest contribution you can make to your children is to model integrity."

Ronald L. Holechek, LTC, USAR (Ret.)
U.S. Military Ministry Director, The Navigators

"Not unlike most men, I entered this life with a desire to make an impact on my world—to be successful. As I've matured and tried to articulate my personal code of conduct, I've come to realize that moving from success to significance has been a journey filled with many twists and turns. Ultimately, however, it has brought me to the conviction that all of life must be centered on the Person of Jesus Christ.

"A corresponding conviction is that developing Christ-like character is extremely important. Ralph Waldo Emerson once penned these words: 'What lies behind us and what lies before us are tiny matters compared to what lies within us.' Two character qualities in particular have greatly guided and impacted my life: integrity and love. Becoming a man of integrity has meant fostering a core commitment and desire that my habits be congruent with my values, and my words be consistent with my actions. Above all, it means that I endeavor to love Christ with passion, trust Christ in everything, and follow Christ with focused devotion.

"In like manner, I Cor. 13:2 affirms the importance of love: 'If I had the gift of prophecy, and if I knew all the mysteries of the future and knew everything about everything, but didn't love others, what good would I be?' This verse serves as a continual reminder that love needs to be one of the hallmarks of my life. A life centered on Christ marked by integrity and a genuine love for others—now that's true significance."

Sam Jacobs
Bishop, Alexandria, LA

"Mother Theresa of Calcutta once said: 'God doesn't need our successes but wants our faithfulness.' The world measures a person's worth by technical achievements and material possessions. God measures a person's faithfulness in the midst of daily struggles and difficulties of life.

"Someone, many years ago, shared a motto of life which I have tried to implement in my journey. 'Do what you are supposed to do, when you are supposed to do it, the way you are supposed to do it, to the best of your ability for the love of God.'

"I am not interested in pleasing anyone except God, not so that He can love me, but that I can love Him for the love He has already poured out on me."

David Jeremiah
Turning Point Ministries
Shadow Mountain Community Church

"God has a blueprint plan for our lives, written in the palm of His hand. 'See, I have inscribed you on the palms of My hands; your walls are continually before Me' (Isaiah 49:16).

"The Bible says we do not have because we do not ask. Therefore, if we don't know God's direction in our lives, we simply ought to try asking Him for guidance. By prayerfully seeking direction, surrendering completely to Him, and listening attentively to His will (whatever it may be), what once seemed mysterious and unrecognizable will become amazingly clear.

"When we follow God's will and live according to His divine plan, our vision expands, and we begin to look at life not in terms of what *we can do,* but what *God can do through us.* We soon realize that nothing can distract, destroy, discourage, disappoint, or defeat us when we follow God's direction.

"When He shows the path for you to follow, then trust Him and His plan with all your heart. Charge down the path with all you've got. Pursue His will with a passion. You'll quickly find that there's no more fulfilling, peaceful, and thankful place to be in this life than soundly in the center of God's will."

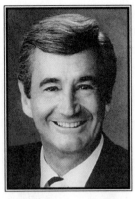

D. James Kennedy
Coral Ridge Presbyterian Church
President, Evangelism Explosion International

"Our first responsibility is to be refashioned in God's image as an on-going process—which must begin, of course, with repentance and faith in Jesus Christ as the Son of God and Savior of the world. After that, we are obligated to bring as many other people as possible into the same relationship with the Lord. Then we are to take all the potentialities of this world and surrender them by doing God's will on earth as it is in heaven. Anything less means that we are falling short of the purpose for which we were created. It is true that the unexamined life is not worth living, and that it will inevitably lead us into conflict with the God we were meant to know, to serve, and to enjoy."

Woodrow Kroll
Back to the Bible

"I believe only what touches eternity is truly significant. Therefore, it is my habit to go to the end and work backward in every endeavor in life. For me, as a Christian, that means beginning each day at the Judgment Seat of Christ. It is only when I start there that I am able to hold my daily activities to an eternal standard. And since that standard belongs to God, it is both high and holy. I have never known God to use an unclean vessel for anything of eternal significance, and that means I must offer every moment of my life to Him with clean hands and a pure heart. I have all eternity to enjoy the rewards of this life, but only a short time to prepare for all eternity."

Rabbi Daniel Lapin
Toward Tradition

"Don't we all yearn for a little red button that is clearly marked, 'press here for the answer and solution to any questions or problem?' That is why most of us respond with interest when someone says, 'There's one thing I can tell you' or 'Here is the secret that I have discovered.' Unfortunately, there is no such red button and very few of life's challenges can be neatly solved with one pithy piece of advice.

"There are, however, three vital questions which can be used as a sort of emergency road kit; three questions to ask yourself at every one of life's many crossroads; three questions that will usually direct and guide you reliably. Here they are:

1. Where did you come from?
2. Where are you headed?
3. What is the best way to get from (1) to (2)?

"These three questions could use some explanation. You see, asking where you came from is a good way to ascertain just who you really are. Fools constantly seek their identities, hoping tomorrow will suddenly yield that answer. The wise realize that they are linked to the reality of the values, hopes, and beliefs that brought them into existence. The motto, 'Be true to yourself' is just a selfish way of justifying an elastic conscience. 'Be true to where you came from' is a constant reminder not to betray your past.

"The second question constantly reminds you to keep your real long-term goals in the forefront of your mind. Almost every destructive decision you ever make will come about only after you decide to ignore your real long-term goals in favor of some short-term interest.

"Finally, question number three motivates one to use the precious present instant to bring to life the values of one's past in order to make tomorrow's dreams the reality. These three questions are really just a warning that we do not live only in the present. Life is lived most successfully when our present actions are designed to bridge the gap between our pasts and our futures."

Eddie L. Long
New Birth Missionary Baptist Church

"The greatest advice for life today must come from an understanding of whose we are and why we were created. God is our creator. He is the eternal Lord, Master, and King who has a plan for everything and everyone; He acts and sees generationally. And He is not limited by anything—not history, current circumstances, or time. The main focus of our lives must rest in the answer to the question, 'When I die, would it even matter that I was born?' In this thought, our eternal destiny and temporal purposes come together. We were in eternity past with God. We were born into time to complete a work for Him after which we will return to Him in eternity. What you do in time will determine your position in

eternity. But, we must not and cannot be selfish with this understanding. We must live our lives always keeping in mind the legacy
we will leave to our grandchildren and great grandchildren. We
have the opportunity to be a blessing, both now and after we're
gone.

"Everything we do today has generational implications for
tomorrow. From serving in the Body and the local community to
economic stewardship, from participating in the political process to
eating right and exercising, we are held accountable for the level of
our personal and corporate stewardship. We must understand that
we pass on knowledge, tendencies, training, and habits to our children in the form of wealth. Riches are the material possessions and
money that we have accumulated and passed on. The foundation
for the future generations to build upon and continue to go higher and higher, depend on the wealth and riches we leave behind.
This is God's ideal for us. The biggest travesty in the Body of Christ
is that each successive generation must start all over because no real
wealth and riches were passed on for them to build upon.

"We must also understand the key difference between destiny
and purpose. We, the Body of Christ, tend to seek our purpose.
Purpose is what you do today but *destiny* is what God thought
about you and called you to fulfill in eternity past. Everything has
a purpose, even inanimate objects. Imagine a chair. It has a purpose—to be sat upon. When it gets old, it will be replaced with
another chair, and no one will remember the previous one. Destiny,
on the other hand, cannot be forgotten. It will be remembered and
passed on to future generations. Therefore, I must live my life—we
all must live our lives—with our destiny in mind.

"Bill Russell of the Boston Celtics had a quote over his locker.
It said, 'The game is scheduled, I must play it so I might as well
win.' If there is one nugget of truth, one shred of wisdom, one
piece of advice for life, it could be summed up in this: 'Life is scheduled, you must live it so you might as well win.' Our ultimate success is not determined merely by what we do now but by the state
of the lives we've blessed, and how much better off we've left those
who follow us when we are gone."

Max Lucado
Pastor, Author, Oak Hills Church of Christ

He offered this advice from his book *A Gentle Thunder*: "God's love never ceases. Never. Though we spurn Him. Ignore Him. Reject Him. Despise Him. Disobey Him. He will not change. Our evil cannot diminish His love. Our goodness cannot increase it. Our faith does not earn it any more than our stupidity jeopardizes it. God doesn't love us less if we fail. He doesn't love us more if we succeed. God's love never ceases."

John C. Maxwell
Author, Speaker and Founder of INJOY, Inc.

"Every person can make his or her life count. It doesn't matter where you start; the important thing is where you finish. As you use your gifts and seize opportunities, live a life of principle. And remember that success is:
- Knowing God and His purpose for your life
- Growing to reach your maximum potential
- Sowing seeds that benefit others

"Pursue a life of significance, and success is practically inevitable."

Bill McCartney
Founder and CEO of Promise Keepers

Coach McCartney offered this advice from his book, *Go the Distance*: "Being broken by God is key to everything! You may ask, what does it mean to be broken? The apostle Paul gave us the definition: 'Godly sorrow brings repentance that leads to salvation and leaves no regret, but worldly sorrow brings death.'

"A heart broken by 'godly sorrow' is beautiful in God's sight. Such a heart is indignant to pride, repentant of sin, and undone by its own depravity. Such a heart is earnest and eager to see justice done. Jesus told us, 'My grace is sufficient for you, for my power is made perfect in weakness' (2 Cor. 12:9 NIV). Brokenness is God's prerequisite for the release of His power. God pours out his Spirit in fullness as we're emptied and broken."

Alfred C. McClure
President, Seventh-Day Adventist Church in North America

"The most important trait in a leader who would be significant is the trait of integrity. In the Seventh-Day Adventist faith we have a saying: 'The greatest want of the world is the want of people who stand for the right though the heavens fall.' That's integrity. First, knowing what is right; and then, second, doing what is right no matter what the consequences.

"Then integrity should be combined with love, the great Christian principle. Jesus said we should love God with all our hearts, and love our neighbors as ourselves. Christians have not always expressed this principle of love well, but it must be a characteristic of a leader.

"Integrity practiced by a person who cares deeply about the welfare of others will produce a leader of significance."

Josh McDowell
Author, Speaker

"Being a godly father to my children is the single most important job I can fulfill. Fatherhood may be the most frightening job in the world, but it is certainly the most rewarding. You can become the father your children need by approaching fathering from a positive, optimistic perspective, looking at growth as a series of small steps taken over a lifetime, and lastly, determining to dedicate yourself to the privilege and responsibility of fathering."

Jack McQueeney
The Navigators
Executive Director, Eagle Lake Camp

"One of the most influential men in my life (a spiritual mentor of mine) once shared Hebrews 13:7 with me; it stays with me to this day as I pass it on to the men I meet with: 'Remember your leaders, who spoke the word of God to you.' Consider the outcome of their way of life and imitate their faith.

"To remember is to think about and not to ignore; to ask questions in order to gain fresh perspective...then to consider and imitate their faith. To finish well you must live well. Romans 10:17 is a big part of this, 'Consequently, faith comes from hearing the message, and the message is heard through the word of Christ.' It seems to me that it's impossible to have faith in God without a word from God. I believe the bottom line is in making time to be with Jesus in His Word; and, as a result, you'll be in tune with what He desires of your leadership."

Dennis M. Mulder
President, The Bible League

"Character, competency, and a servant attitude are three indispensables of life if you are to be successful, let alone live a life of significance. In order to have people trust you, you need to be a person of solid character—a person of integrity—a person whose walk matches their talk. People who live a life of significance base their lives on a set of unchanging principles. I've found mine in God's Word.

"However, in addition, we need to be people of competency in our chosen field of labor. Therefore, continuing education and extensive reading are a must. Few of us would want an incompetent carpenter to build our home—even if he were a person of solid character.

"Finally, we must have the biblical attitude of servanthood in all we do. Christ needs to be our example. We need to truly understand the biblical paradox. It is in dying that we live, in giving that we receive, in loving we are loved.

"Be trustworthy, be an expert in your field and act only to serve. In so doing, you will make a significant difference."

Luis Palau

Luis Palau Evangelistic Association

"Two events revolutionized my life. First, when I was 12 years old, I asked Jesus Christ into my heart. The next occurred nearly 15 years later when I finally understood that it's futile trying to please God in our own strength. But, praise the Lord, He is pleased to live in us! All the resources of Jesus Christ are entirely at our disposal. Because He indwells us, all that is Christ's is ours.

"The Lord desires that we live today enjoying the fact that, 'It's not I, but Christ who lives in me' (Galatians 2:20). Imagine how different your life would be if you were completely, totally filled with God Himself. No area of your life would be untouched. You would love God so much more deeply. You would care so much more about others. And you would have such compassion for those who don't love God yet. Even with the weaknesses we all have, the power would be tremendous.

"Our whole purpose is that God takes over more and more of our lives, that He molds His character in us, and that we become like His Son, Jesus Christ. What really counts is this: Does God run my life? Is He in control? Or am I trying to run the show?"

Paul Pettit
Dynamic Dads Ministry

"Significance may go unnoticed until one's son or daughter arrives on the playing field of life. Upon what was the dinner conversation normally centered? How did the man act when none but the children were watching? Was the children's mother elevated to her proper place? All of these outcomes live on after individual accomplishments. For the actions of his offspring go on and on through several cycles waiting either to be corrected or strengthened by an equal or greater hand."

Randy Phillips
Vice President, Promise Keepers

"One of my favorite quotes is 'He who is enslaved by the compass has the freedom of the seas.' Is there such a thing as a real life magnetic north?

"When life leads us into the depression of a heavy fog is there some kind of focal point where we can regain perspective? I believe the answer is yes. The solution is the most generally understood yet most neglected among all believers. Life's magnetic north is allowing the insatiable hunger and thirst of our need to be in touch with the person of Jesus Christ to be the most distinctive discipline of our daily lives.

- The greatest challenge in life is to know the word of Christ.
- The greatest crisis in life is the relational bankruptcy between the disciple and the Discipler.
- The greatest opportunity in life is to receive in and through our soul the mercy, grace, peace, and transforming power of Christ in us.

'Christ in you, the hope of glory. Him we preach, warning every man and teaching every man in all wisdom, that we may present every man perfect in Christ Jesus' (Col. 1:27-28)."

Bishop Phillip H. Porter
All Nations Pentecostal Center

"Saint Matthew 6:33 holds the creed and code of my life: 'But seek ye first the kingdom of God, and His righteousness; and all these things shall be added unto you.'

"This foundation that never fades away has always been critical for me. In this verse, I find a foundation immovable, steadfast, and prioritized. I also find an undefeatable relationship of 1) God's everlasting Kingdom, 2) His righteousness, and 3) my surrendered life, which equals an unconquerable trio. The promise of the Holy Bible, especially this verse, coupled with Rudyard Kipling's poem, 'IF' has sustained me over these 60 years. I would highly recommend them to any and all children, youth and young adults."

William Prince
General Superintendent, Church of the Nazarene

"The hope for a future is in a sincere and true faith in God. God is the Creator and sustainer of all creation. He sent His Son, Jesus Christ, to become the Savior of a fallen humanity. Jesus comes as the Way, the Truth, and the Life to bring redemption and reconciliation.

"God has revealed Himself and His love for humanity through His word, the Bible. This Word presents to us the plan of God for salvation, the love of God, and the moral principles of God. Obedience to His Word and His will for our lives sets us free.

"God is love; God is holy. God has extended His love and holiness to us. Jesus said that the greatest commandment is to love God with all our heart, mind, and strength, and our neighbor as ourself. These are life-sustaining characteristics."

Ramesh Richard
RREACH International,
Dallas Theological Seminary

"First, *decide on your passion* in life—what should be your first love? If you have multiple passions, you will be ripped to pieces internally, resulting in a fragmented, random life. If anything other than the Lord Jesus Christ is your first love, you will fall into idolatry. You won't know how to balance your life. Your family, your work, your ministry, your interests—all of these are crucial dimensions of your life. But they must not be your passion.

"Next, *identify your mission* in life—what should you do repeatedly? Your mission is not your vocation or job. Broadly speaking, your mission is the same as every other Christian's: to make God look good and His Christ well known. Your unique mission is how you personally advance that divine storyline, for God will receive the glory He is due from His creation by making Christ well-known on earth.

"Finally, *pursue a vision* for your life—what difference should your life make in the world for God? Vision pursues a changed-for-the-better state of affairs. As you increasingly arrange your life around the Lord Jesus Christ (your passion) and better understand His calling on your life (your mission), develop a sensitivity to the world about you. Listen to Him for direction in life, and then follow it."

Oral Roberts
Evangelist, Chancellor, Oral Roberts University

"Honesty and integrity are very important if you want to have credibility in your life. I found it always pays. When I was asking the Lord for forgiveness the night I accepted Him as my Lord and Savior, He brought to my mind the law books I had taken when I lived in a lawyer's home during my high school years. I had been reading the lawyer's books on law and since he had died and I was so interested in law, I just took the books with me when I left. His widow would have never known I took the books if I hadn't told her, but that night when those books came rolling up in front of me, I said, 'Yes, Lord, I'll take the books back and tell the lady I took them!'

"Several weeks after I gave my heart to Jesus, I went to the lawyer's house and gave his widow the books and explained to her that I had taken the books, but now that I had been forgiven by God, I wanted her forgiveness, too. She gladly gave it and said to me, 'Oral, God is going to do something special with you. You are on the right road.' That was the beginning of honesty which has been my policy all these years. I've had opportunity many times in my life to cheat, but I've found that God blesses me and blesses people through me when I tell the whole truth and live an honest life."

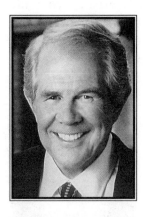

Pat Robertson
The Christian Broadcasting Network

"My personal creed is that the chief aim of my life is to bring glory to Almighty God and His Son, Jesus Christ, and to do whatever I am able to help others to know Him better.

"I believe that true greatness comes from serving. The more that we are able to serve, the more that we enter into true significance in life. I define success as the progressive realization of worthwhile goals; but true significance only comes from that which we are able to do to help others."

James Robison
LIFE Outreach International

"Perhaps one of the saddest issues in ministry is that of succeeding publicly while failing privately. The Lord God must be the center of our lives. As we love Him with all our heart, soul, mind, and strength, we will experience the real possibility of loving our neighbors as ourselves. Herein is the Father's love most clearly revealed. He expresses His heart through us and extends His hands through ours. I have found that the more we love Him, the more clearly He reveals His heart to us. Everything in His heart, however, is not our personal part of responsibility in life. Seeking to discover our part in His heart and yielding to His Holy Spirit's divine enabling is the ultimate experience."

Dave Roever
Dave Roever Evangelistic Association

"Life is not fair, and all who live long enough to discover the reality of this truth also live long enough to discover that the really big question of life is not, is it fair, but rather, how will one deal with life's inequities?

"As I watched nearly half the skin of my body float down the Vam Co Ta River in Vietnam in 1969, I knew that there was not going to be an easy road to recovery if there was to be any recovery. Sixty pounds of flesh was blown off in the explosion, but the damage was to be relegated only to my body...not my soul. My love for life was never at risk. The scars would be on the outside only. It is my opinion that scars are nothing to be ashamed of, anyway.

"So, what is a scar? It is evidence of these things: One, that you got hurt. All wounds leave a scar when they heal, which brings me to the second point about a scar. It is evidence that you not only got hurt but that you got over it! Getting over it is part of the spice of life. The joy of success. The third, and not least important, point is that a man with a scar is easy to believe. He wears his evidence on his body that he has been there and done that. In other words, the scar is his right of passage . . . his right to say, 'I know how you feel!' At that moment, tragedy is turned into triumph and the life of that man is turned from success to significance!"

Adrian Rogers
Love Worth Finding Ministries,
Pastor, Bellevue Baptist Church

"The most important ingredient in life is integrity. Integrity, however, does not deal in the great, major issues of life but in the small ones. Our Lord said, 'He that is faithful in that which is least, is faithful also in much; and he that is unjust in the least is unjust also in much' (Luke 16:10).

"Everything big is made up of something small. The ocean is made up of millions of drops of water. The human body of individual cells. A mountain avalanche is made up of snowflakes.

"The scripture does not say that if a man is unfaithful in that which is least that he might also be unfaithful in that which is much. He already is unfaithful in much. One who would steal five dollars is as unfaithful as a man who would steal five million.

"When young preachers ask me for a word about their ministry, I give them one word—integrity. And then I go on to say that this means faithfulness in the small things. Be scrupulously honest. Be kind. Be faithful. Be obedient in the smaller matters, and you will be amazed at what happens with the larger ones."

Father Michael Scanlan, TOR
President, Franciscan University of Steubenville

"If you ask my friends, they'll tell you, as they frequently told me, that I have been unqualified for most positions I've held from secondary school on. They said I was too short and too slow to play high school quarterback; too inexperienced to lead the legal office at Andrews Air Force Base as staff judge advocate; and they simply laughed when I—who had never served on a faculty—became academic dean at Steubenville.

"I didn't succeed at these and many other challenges because of my qualifications; I succeeded because God made up for my lack. The words of Jesus in John's Gospel define my condition, 'Apart from me you can do nothing' (John 15:5). Believing these words, consecrating my life and work to God, and relying on His Holy Spirit have enabled me to overcome obstacles and achieve goals even though I wasn't 'qualified.'

"Despite what others say about your qualifications, you too can succeed as a spouse, parent, business or professional leader, priest or sister, missionary or minister. Once you decide after testing an inspiration that God has called you to a task, His grace will be sufficient for His power is made perfect in weakness (II Cor. 12:9)."

Wallace Schulz
The Lutheran Hour

"Christianity gives conviction and courage. Saint Paul said, 'I can do all things in Christ who strengthens me' (Phil 4:13). This strength comes from Jesus not simply because He is our example. Rather, this strength comes to us when we are connected to Jesus through God's gift of faith. This strength was also joyously confessed during the Littleton, Colorado, high school massacre. Two days before she was martyred, and quoting from the Apostle Paul's words to the Ephesian Christians, Cassie Bernall wrote about the 'surpassing greatness of His power toward us who believe.' Incredible as it may seem to us, in His Word, God speaks clearly about the power that lives in Christians as being the same power He, as our Father, used to raise His Son Jesus Christ from the dead! (Ephesians 1: 1-19.)"

Gary Smalley
TODAY's FAMILY

"I start every day reaffirming three pillars that form the structure and significance of my life: I highly honor God, others and myself, in that order of priority. Practically, I re-establish my commitment to place God as my highest value and worthy of my highest worship. He is my main source of strength and sustains my existence. Second, I affirm that people are more important than anything material. Lastly, I attach honor to whatever is happening to me, good or bad, through an attitude of thanksgiving. This honoring expression has become natural because I have found that all things do work together for good to those who love God and who continue to love others."

Charles Stanley
In Touch Ministries

"Whatever you may face tomorrow, today, or at some point in the future, you can depend on the fact that God is facing it with you. He will never leave you. One of His greatest desires is for you to become a success by experiencing His joy on a daily basis.

Achieving this begins with a relationship—yours with Him. I would offer this challenge for everyone who longs to reach a degree of success: make intimacy with God your top priority."

Paul D. Stanley
Executive Vice President, The Navigators

"Over the past 40 years there have been many people, events, and circumstances that the sovereign hand of God brought into my life. I have learned that my response to each of these is the primary factor as to how deeply and significantly they have shaped my life. I have learned and am still learning that there are certain life principles that, when followed, always give a deep sense of peace within and result in a life well-lived. These have been particularly important to me in the leadership roles I have played.

"Life Principles: My life, capacities, and opportunities are from God. Therefore, I am grateful, responsible, and accountable to Him for these...to develop and use them for good.

"Trust and respect are the greatest aspects a person and leader can have as he deals with others. They are earned through integrity, good character, and relevant competency. Therefore, I must always be growing, learning, and open to others' contributions.

"People are created by God in His own image and, therefore, have unique capacities and destinies. I must seek to be enriched by all those around me and commit myself to help them become their fullest for God and mankind.

"God is a purposeful God and always acts and creates with purpose. Therefore, I am created for a purpose and must live life to serve Him and others with His purposes in mind. To perform any task without having a sense of purpose is inconsistent with God's creation and ways. He blesses those who operate within His purposes.

"Giving and forgiving are God-like acts of grace. Awareness of how much I have been given and forgiven inspires me to do the same. Therefore, I must endeavor to reflect often on God's and others' grace given to me, and seek to continually extend it to others. Peace and joy are most often manifested internally and externally when this is done."

Roger Staubach
Chairman & CEO The Staubach Company

"My parents were both exemplary Christians. They deserve the credit for establishing a value-system that is the cornerstone of my success.

"One of the strongest memories of how my values were formed and tested occurred when I played Little League Baseball in Cincinnati, Ohio. I really enjoyed playing first base, but our coach decided I should be the catcher. Catcher was just not a position I wanted to play because of having to wear all that heavy gear. It was not as glamorous or exciting as first base. My Dad quickly let me know the coach obviously knew best. Though it might not be what I wanted, it was where I was needed. Dad emphasized it was very important to do my best to help the team succeed; he was adamant that I should work hard at being the best catcher our team ever had.

"Later on during high school, once again I was asked by a coach to change positions. This time it was the football coach; he asked me to give up playing wide-receiver to be quarterback. Having experienced a similar situation and recalling what Dad said,

I was determined to learn the quarterback position in order to become the best quarterback our high school ever had.

"What lessons were learned from those life experiences? 1) It is important and necessary to put forth your best effort to accomplish whatever task is at hand. 2) You may have to do something uncomfortable in order to be successful. These lessons helped in developing and expanding my athletic skills. They taught me the results of perseverance and hard work. They were invaluable in understanding teamwork and respecting the wisdom of leaders and coaches, both on and off the playing field.

"Both my parents instilled their religion, not by preaching, but by living their faith every day throughout their lives. Even as my mother aged and suffered with poor health, witnessing her unrelenting faith continually rejuvenated mine.

"Along with an active faith in Almighty God, the lessons I learned from my beloved parents prepared me for my future—including military service, a career in professional football, and now in commercial real estate. The love and respect my parents had for God, for each other, and for me, enriches my 35-year marriage and family life."

Robert H. Stein
Professor, The Southern Baptist Theological Seminary

"There is a question that I keep in the forefront of my thinking that has provided guidance and direction throughout my life. This question is, 'Is the issue that I am facing worth living and dying for?' This has assisted me in understanding what is ultimately important in life. It is so easy to let secondary and insignificant issues dominate and control life. This question has helped me focus on what is truly important. It is evident that there are many things not worth dying for. Salaries, houses, cars, possessions, etc., are certainly not life and death issues. They are not worth dying for. On the other hand, there *are* things worth dying for: God, family, honor, justice, people in need, etc.

"Another way in which this question has helped me is to prioritize those items for which I want to live. It is not surprising that these tend to be the same things for which I am willing to die. If I do not have anything for which I am willing to die, then it is evident that I have no purpose for which I want to live. A life that has nothing for which it is willing to live and die is ultimately an empty and meaningless life."

Joseph M. Stowell
President, Moody Bible Institute

Dr. Stowell offered this advice from his book, *Perilous Pursuits*: "It is safe to say that there is not an area of life that is unaffected by the primal need for significance. But apart from Christ, the passages through which we normally move to establish and maintain our significance, even when successfully negotiated, most often leave us with a sense of sorrow, loss, and regret.

"Our need for significance is not the culprit. We were built for significance. The culprit is our struggling, stumbling attempts to manufacture our own sense of significance and in the process place at risk that very thing for which we strive, the very people we need and love, the society in which we move, and the cause of Christ for which we have been redeemed.

"We confront perilous results by seeking to fulfill our significance outside of God's plan. This pursuit can only produce regret because it is focused on things other than God, who made us for something more. The tragedy is that so many are searching for significance where it cannot be found, when significance has already been secured for us by Christ.

"Significance is not a search. It is a gift. When we receive full significance in Christ, we are liberated to live His significance through us and to enjoy His significant plans. This is our need. Only when we have been reunited with God through redemption will we discover the significance we were made to enjoy."

Chuck Swindoll
President, Dallas Theological Seminary
Senior Pastor, Stonebriar Community Church

"I take great pride in my service to the nation as a Marine. Just as the motto *'Semper Fidelis'* (always faithful) affected my life so does one's attitude.

"Words can never adequately convey the incredible impact of our attitude toward life. The longer I live, the more convinced I become that life is 10 percent what happens to us and 90 percent how we respond to it.

"I believe the single most significant decision I can make on a day-to-day basis is my choice of attitude. It is more important than my past, my education, my bankroll, my successes or failures, fame or pain, what other people think of me or say about me, my circumstances, or my position. Attitude keeps me going or cripples my progress...fuels my fire or assaults my hope. When my attitude is right, there's no barrier too high, no valley too deep, no dream too extreme, no challenge too great for me."

Thomas E. Trask
General Superintendent, Assemblies of God

"The scriptures state that 'The steps of a righteous man are ordered of the Lord.' If one desires to pattern his life after the purposes of God and to live out those purposes, he will enjoy the fulfillment and the development that the Christian walk affords.

"The scripture further states, '. . .lean not on thine own understanding. In all thy ways acknowledge Him and He shall direct thy paths' (Prov. 3:5-6). We are promised that He will go before us. His help is ours if we will look to Him, and not be endowed with one's own wisdom, but with the wisdom of God. It will lead to a life of joy, a life of service, a life that is well-pleasing to the Lord, and a life that will result in fruitfulness.

"The Christian walk is best *lived out,* instead of *talked out.* It is one of relationship with the Master Himself."

John Trent
Encouraging Words

"Some of the best advice on leadership I've ever received is actually as old as the Old Testament. When the prophet Samuel was given the task of picking the next king, the Lord told him, 'Do not look at his appearance or at the height of his stature...for God sees not as man sees, for man looks at the outward appearance, but the Lord looks at the heart.'

"Historical accounts put Napoleon at 5'4". Audie Murphy, the most decorated soldier of World War II, was 5'5". No matter what the world says, courage and leadership isn't about physical size, 'image,' or looking good. Leadership is, and always has been a heart issue. If you want to understand a man's leadership potential, look at his character and the size of his heart."

Joe White
CEO, Kanakuk-Kanakomo Kamps

"As I look back over an incredibly blessed 25 years of marriage to the greatest woman alive, being a dad to my heroes and four best friends, or attempting to somehow lead a staff of 1800 enthusiastic, kid-loving Christian athletes, I render myself completely incapable. More and more each day my heart is welded to the life of the most amazing man in history, Jesus Christ. He 'gave it up' so that you and I might live in freedom. His creed was simple, yet profound; 'When any human impulse gets in your way, give it up.' If your wife is in need of a shoulder, 'give it up.' If your team is in need of your resources, 'give it up.' If your kids are in need of your time, 'give it up.' If your pride is in need of a fall, 'give it up.' If your bank account sees a hungry child, 'give it up.' If your eyes see a lustful image or your ears hear a lustful sound, 'give it up.' Because (to our amazement always), in giving we receive, in letting go we're filled up, and in dying to ourselves, we are born into eternal life."

George O. Wood
General Secretary, Assemblies of God

"Being is more important than doing. The first question I always asked myself before hiring a member of my pastoral staff team was: 'Would I like other people to become like this person?' What good does it do for a minister to perform tasks superbly if his or her life is poorly lived? Jesus knew the importance of this principle when, as duty number one for the Twelve, He called them to be with Him (Mark 3:14). Additionally, the Lord began the Sermon on the Mount, His inaugural address of the kingdom, by placing eight qualities of being—commonly called, the beatitudes—in front of all other teaching. Why? Because the Christian life must be modeled by those who teach it.

"The good is the eternal enemy of the best. The maturing believer generally does not make choices which are rank evil acts.

The moral and ethical choices involve discriminating between more subtle shades of the good from the best. For example, Martha did the good thing by being busy; but Mary did the best by taking time to sit at Jesus' feet and focus on him (Mark 10:38-42). We can become so distracted trying to do good things that we may fail to carefully evaluate what's the best thing.

"What happens *in* you is more important than what happens *to* you. Life holds many disappointments, losses, injustices, and sorrows. How you respond to these reverses determines the quality of your life. You have no power to change others or adverse circumstances; but you can, with the Lord's help, control your own reaction to these outside pressures. Keep the streams of forgiveness and blessing flowing rather than becoming stagnant with blame and self-pity. Stay better, not bitter.

"What will matter 100 years from now? As a little boy, my mother drilled that into me. Every time I would be upset about something, she would say, 'Georgie, it won't matter 100 years from now.' I realize now that mother was right. One hundred years from now it will not matter what kind of house you live in, clothes you wear, or type of automobile you drive. What will matter is if you loved the Lord with all your heart, mind, soul, and strength, and your neighbor as yourself. What will matter is your care for family and the cause of Christ. 'Only one life, 'twill soon be past, only what's done for Christ will last.'"

George B. Wood
Chaplain, 82nd Airborne Div. Assn., 505th PIR, WWII, 4 combat jumps

"When my mother first sent me out into the world, she gave me this challenge: 'Do not pray for an easy life. Pray to be a stronger man. Do not pray for tasks equal to your powers. Pray for powers equal to your tasks. Then the doing of your works shall be no miracle, but you shall be a miracle.'

"These words of Philip Brooks sum up the attitude of the airborne 'trooper' in peace and in war: 'I went with them. We prayed to be stronger men. They were! I was!'

"The soldier's scripture is from Ephesians 6:11. Listen to it: 'Put on the whole armor of God, so that you may be able to stand against the wiles of the devil.' Our creed is to be found in the armor of God. 'Our struggle is not against enemies of blood and flesh but against the cosmic powers of this present darkness, against spiritual forces of evil.' This scripture will give all of us our code of conduct."

Ravi K. Zacharias
President, Ravi Zacharias International
Ministries

"Ironically in the New Testament, the word 'leader' hardly ever occurs, but the word 'servant' occurs numerous times. That alone ought to give pause, for the New Testament contains the words of One who has earned a greater following than any other person in history. I am afraid that, over the years, I have seen so many who want to lead, yet very few who understand what it means to serve people as we lead. Any one who looks to leadership for power and prestige while ignoring the value of every individual who works alongside will ultimately end up with merely an office and not the affection and respect of his or her colleagues. That is why the essence of good leadership is that of a relationship that earns respect and not power that commands compliance."

Colonel Jim Coy
U.S. Army Reserve

"Since the first edition of this book was published, I've often been asked to give my advice about a creed or a code of conduct for life. The following is what I share: Always seek to do what is right. With every decision, make a conscious effort to do the right thing. Frequently we have to choose between a more difficult right and an easier wrong. The right decisions pay big dividends!

"My thoughts about success and significance are: Any time we affect a positive change in someone's life, we are successful. More importantly, any time we affect a positive spiritual change in someone's life, we attain significance. Success is temporal; significance is eternal."

About Colonel Jim Coy

Colonel Jim Coy is a medical consultant for the U.S. Army Special Operations Command. He served two years as the national president of the Special Operations Medical Association and as the national surgeon of the Reserve Officers Association. He lectures both nationally and internationally on combat trauma medicine and his ground-breaking research on lightweight x-ray equipment.

Dr. Coy has served with numerous Special Forces and Special Operations units. He served with the 3rd Group Army Special Forces (AIRBORNE) in the 1991 Gulf War. He has received a myriad of military honors, awards, and badges including the Legion of Merit, the Combat Medical Badge, and the prestigious "A" designation—the highest recognition of the Army Medical Department.

He battled with cancer from 1978-1989 with four major surgeries during which portions of his lower throat and jawbone were removed. Today he is considered cured.

Jim and his wife Vicki have three children: Tim, Tricia, and Joshua. His family is extremely important to him. He has a vision to see men become spiritual leaders and stand strong for their families. Colonel Coy is very active in Promise Keepers and Prime Time (an interdenominational group for men) and is the Men's Ministry director at his home church.

Today, Jim desires to develop a ministry to military and former military men and frequently speaks to community, church, and military groups across the United States.